FOULA ISLE SHETLAND ISLANDS

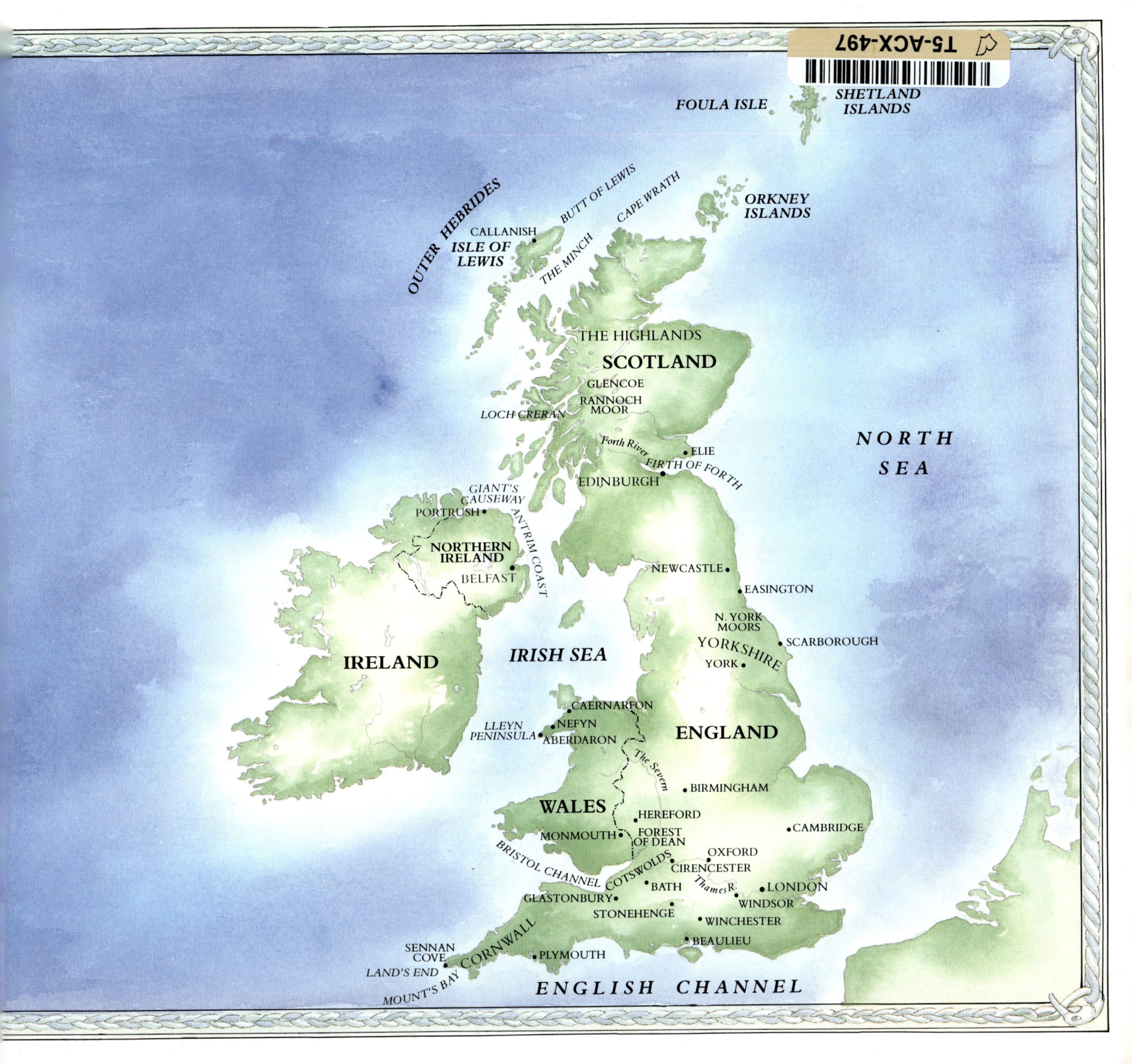

OUTER HEBRIDES
CALLANISH
ISLE OF LEWIS
BUTT OF LEWIS
THE MINCH
CAPE WRATH
ORKNEY ISLANDS

THE HIGHLANDS
SCOTLAND
GLENCOE
RANNOCH MOOR
LOCH CRERAN
Forth River
• ELIE
FIRTH OF FORTH
• EDINBURGH

NORTH SEA

GIANT'S CAUSEWAY
PORTRUSH •
ANTRIM COAST
NORTHERN IRELAND
• BELFAST

NEWCASTLE •
• EASINGTON
N. YORK MOORS
• SCARBOROUGH
YORKSHIRE
• YORK

IRELAND

IRISH SEA

CAERNARFON
• NEFYN
LLEYN PENINSULA
• ABERDARON
ENGLAND

The Severn
• BIRMINGHAM
WALES
• HEREFORD
MONMOUTH •
FOREST OF DEAN
• CAMBRIDGE
OXFORD
COTSWOLDS CIRENCESTER
BRISTOL CHANNEL
BATH
Thames R.
• LONDON
GLASTONBURY
STONEHENGE
WINDSOR
WINCHESTER
• BEAULIEU
SENNAN COVE
CORNWALL
• PLYMOUTH
LAND'S END
MOUNT'S BAY

ENGLISH CHANNEL

PORTRAIT OF
GREAT BRITAIN
AND
NORTHERN IRELAND

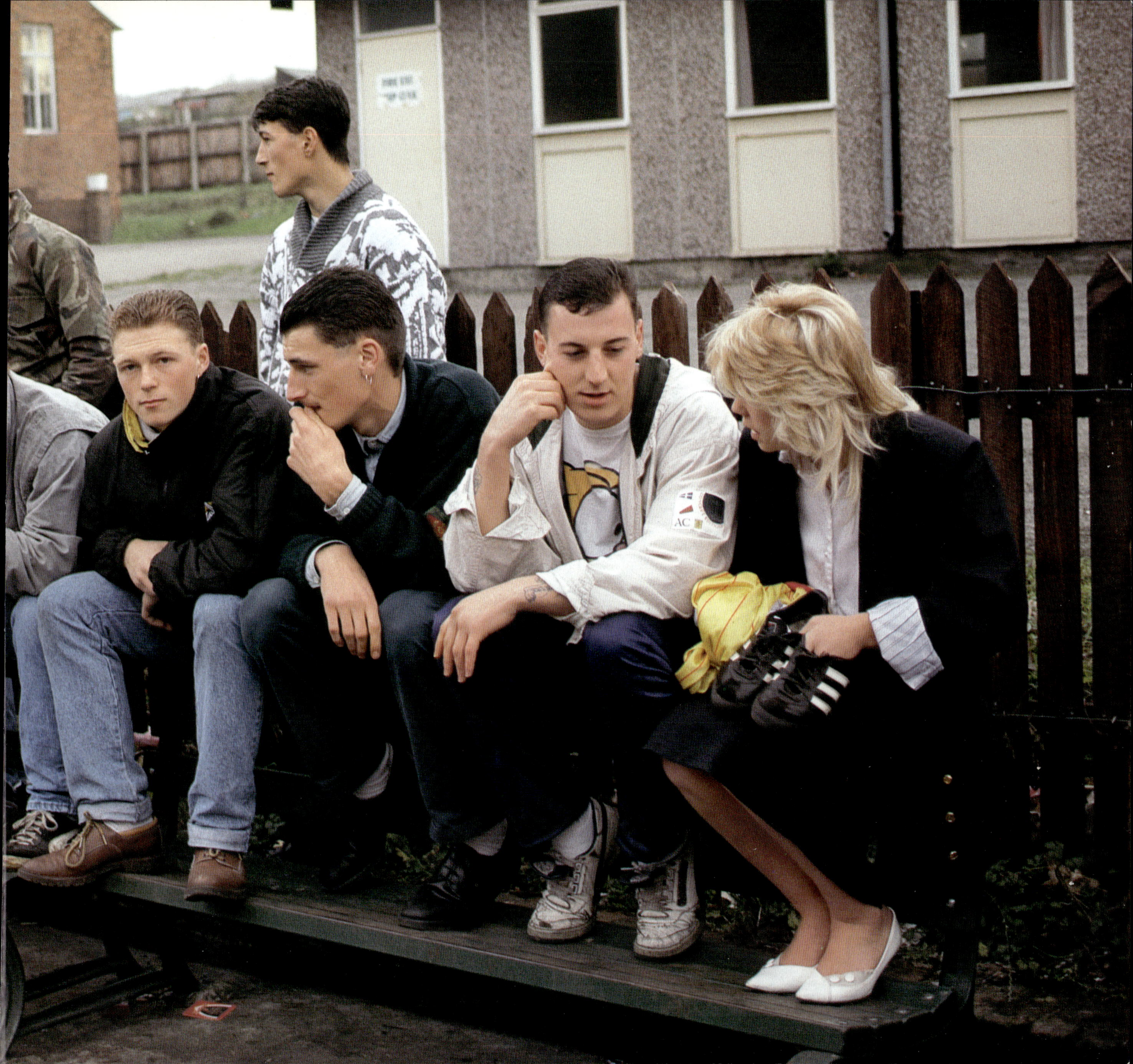
AC

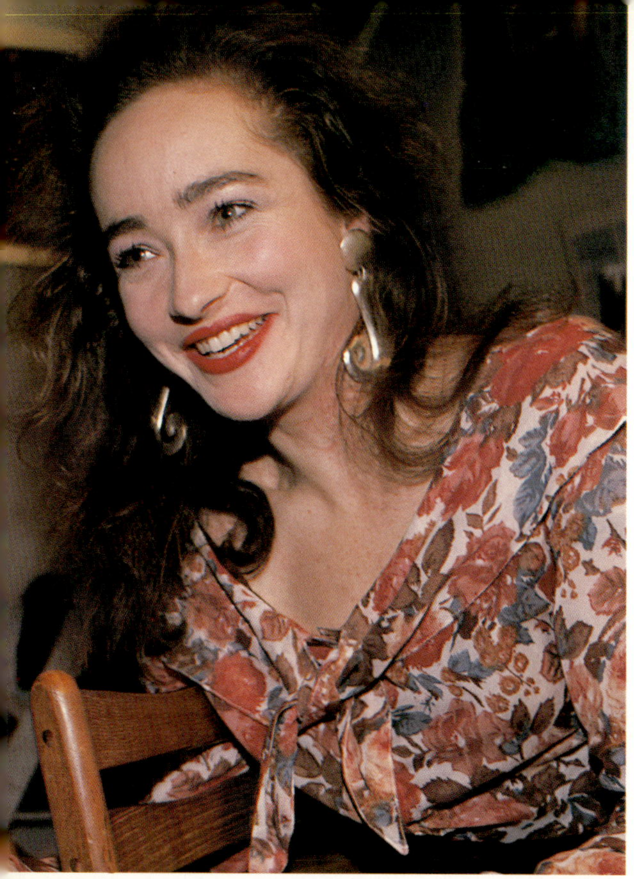
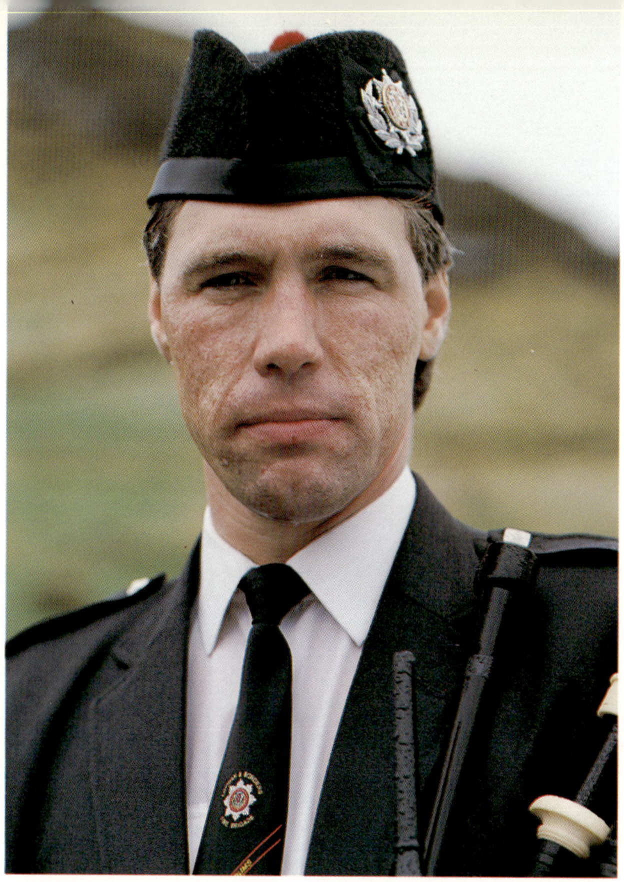
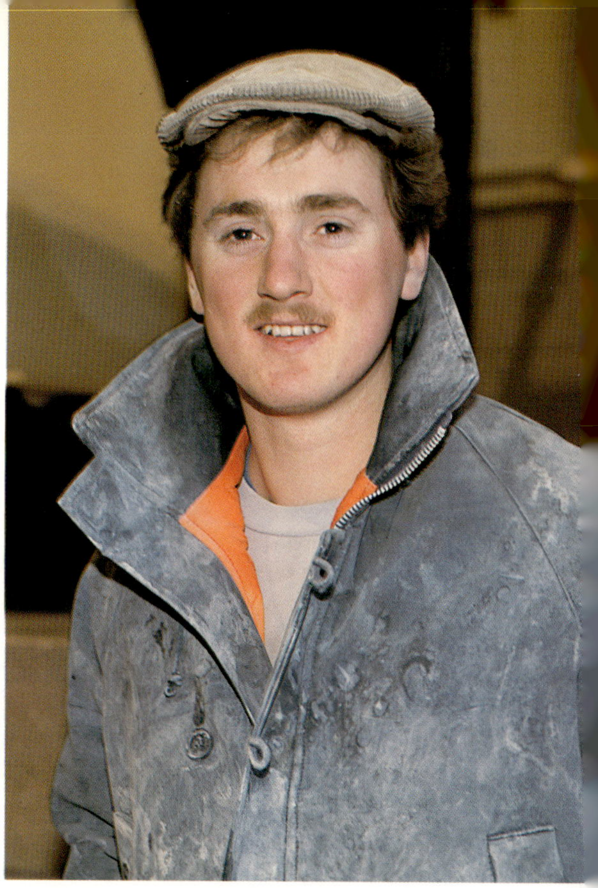
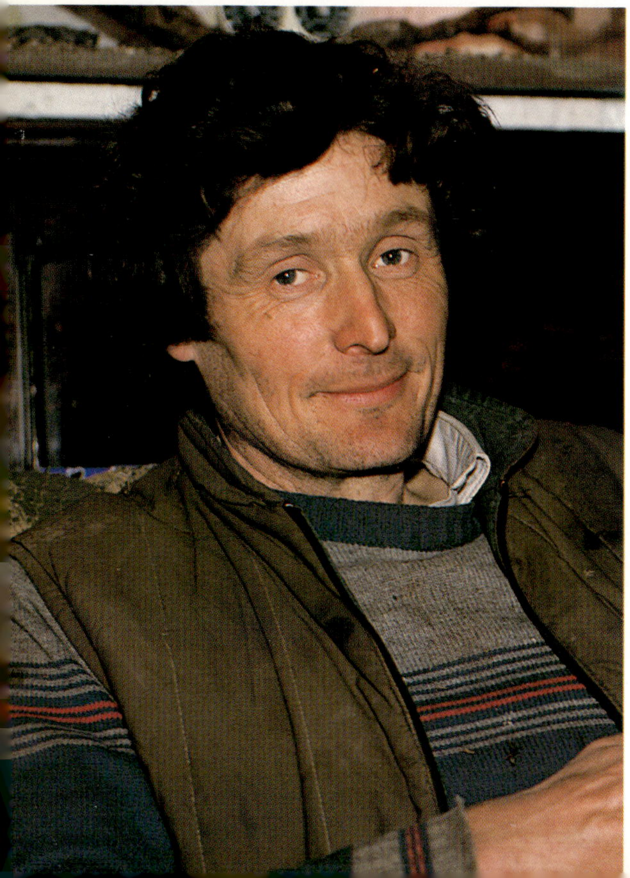
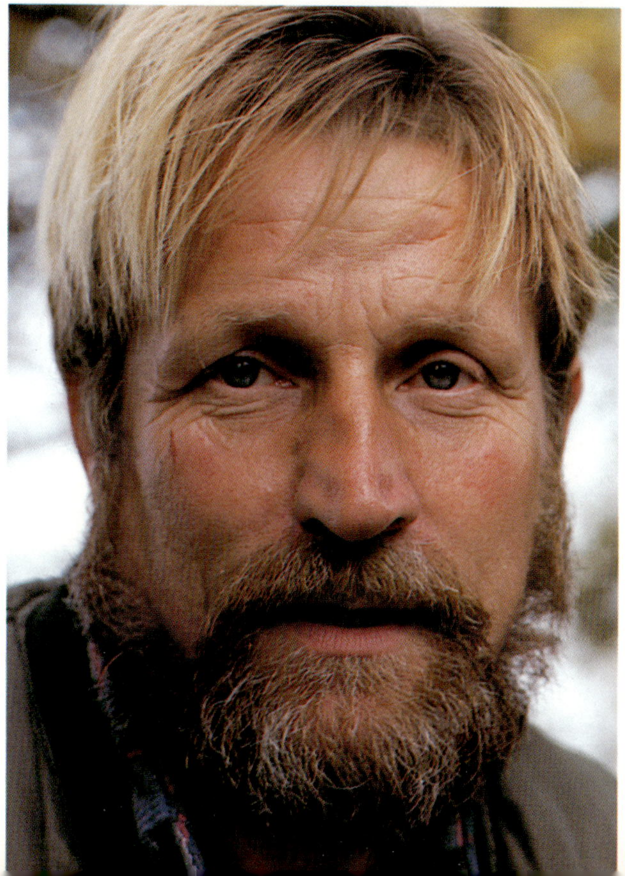
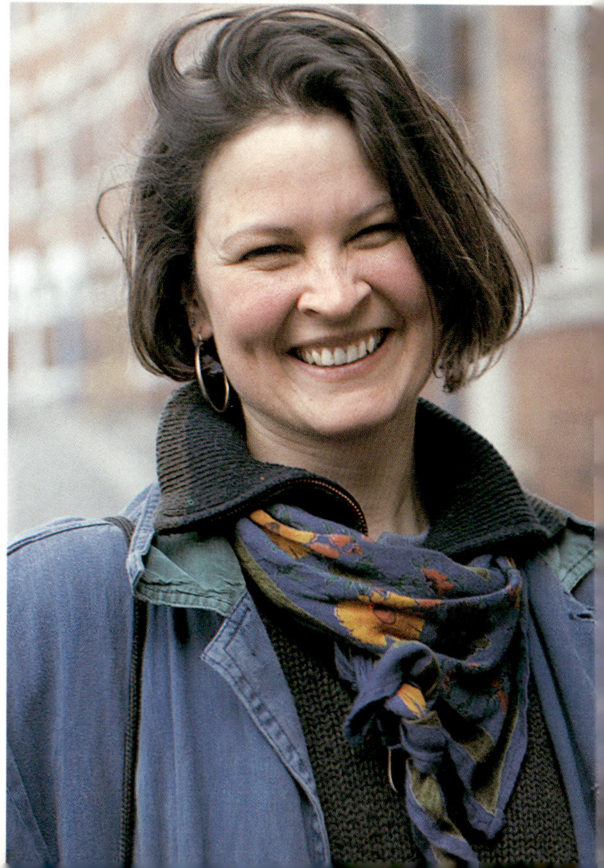

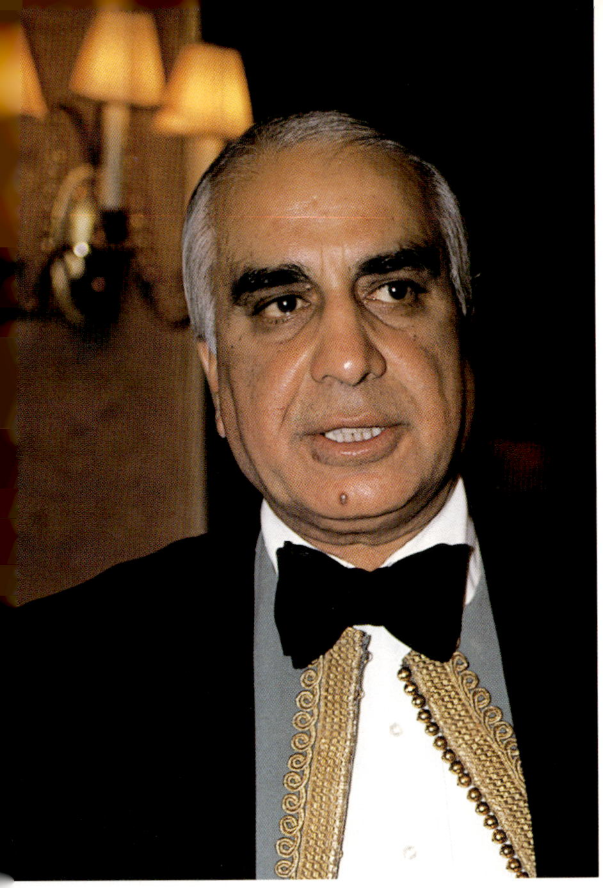
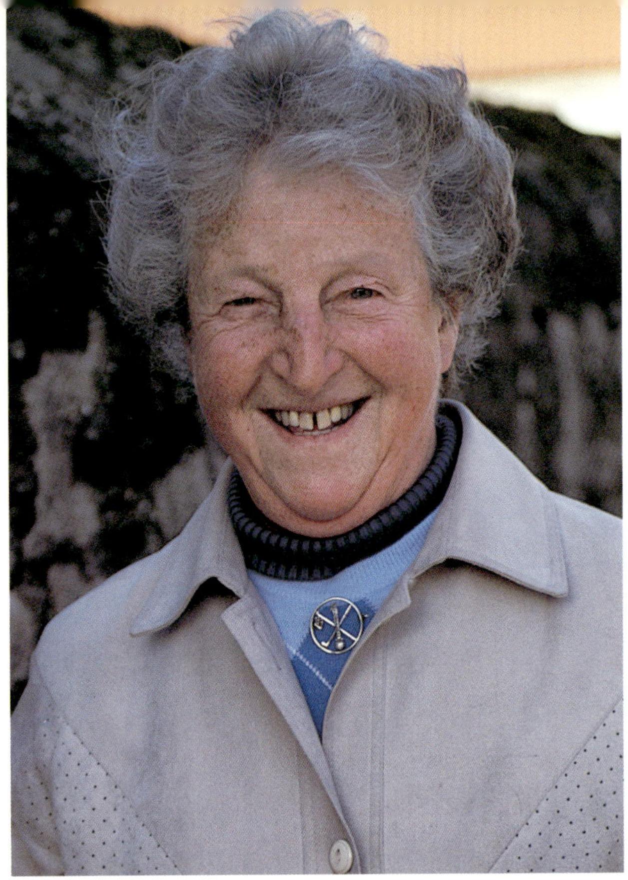
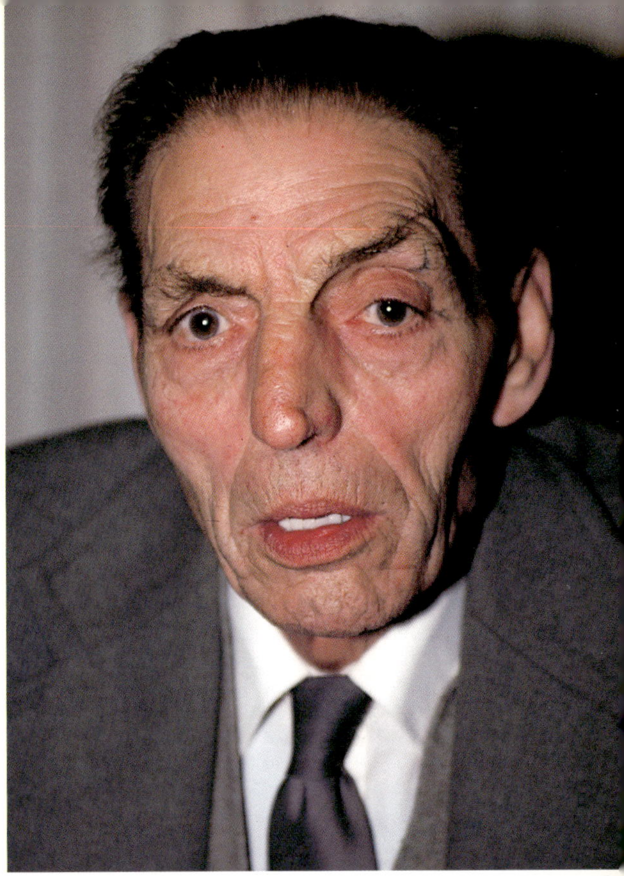
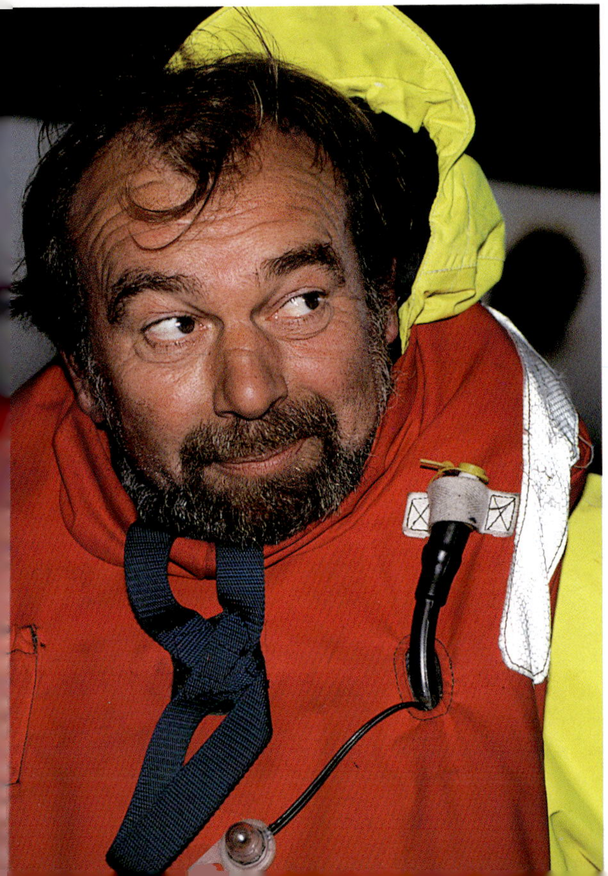
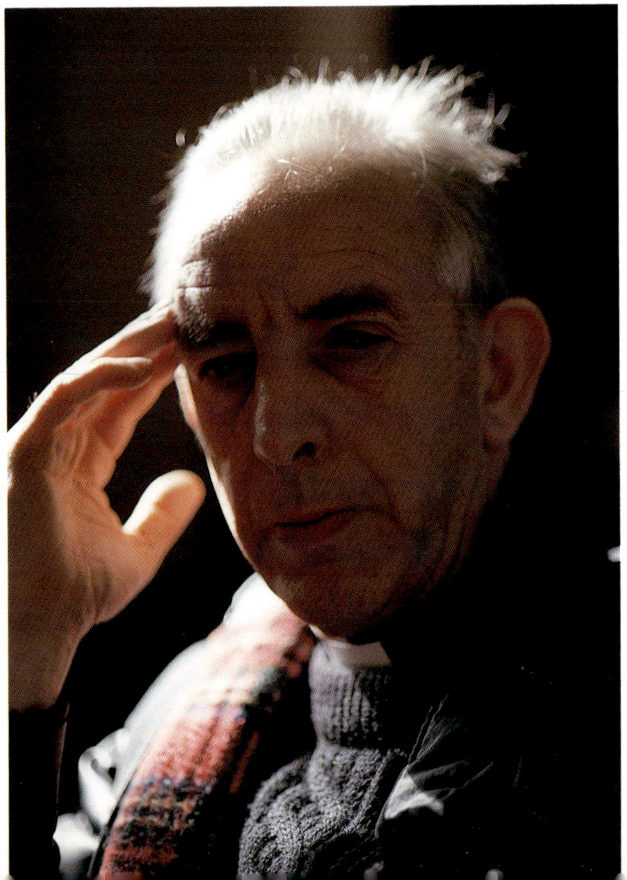
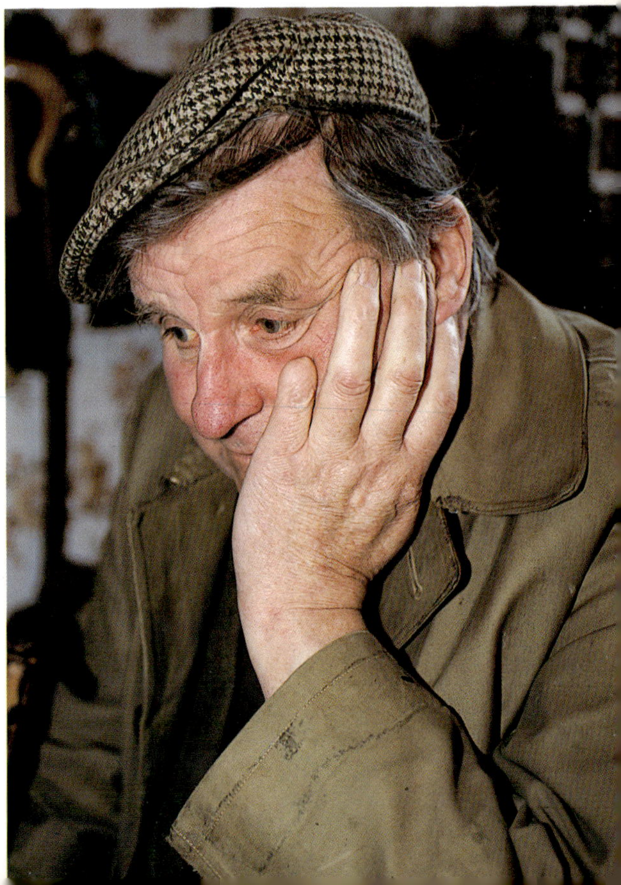

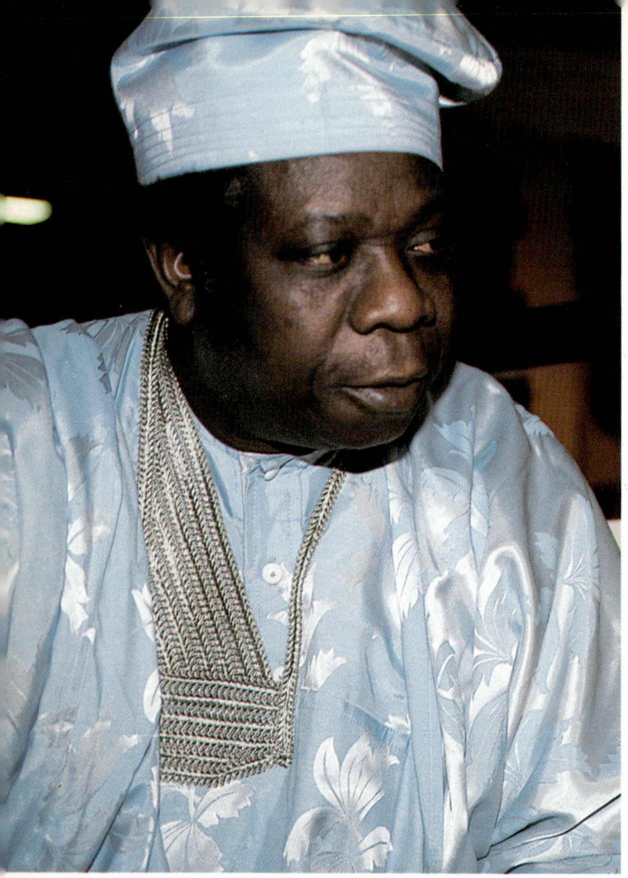
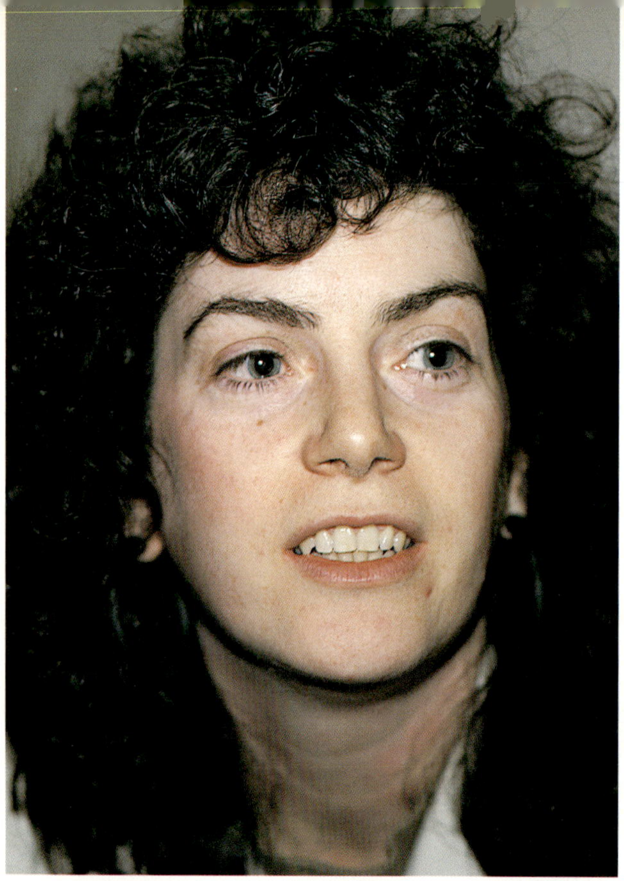
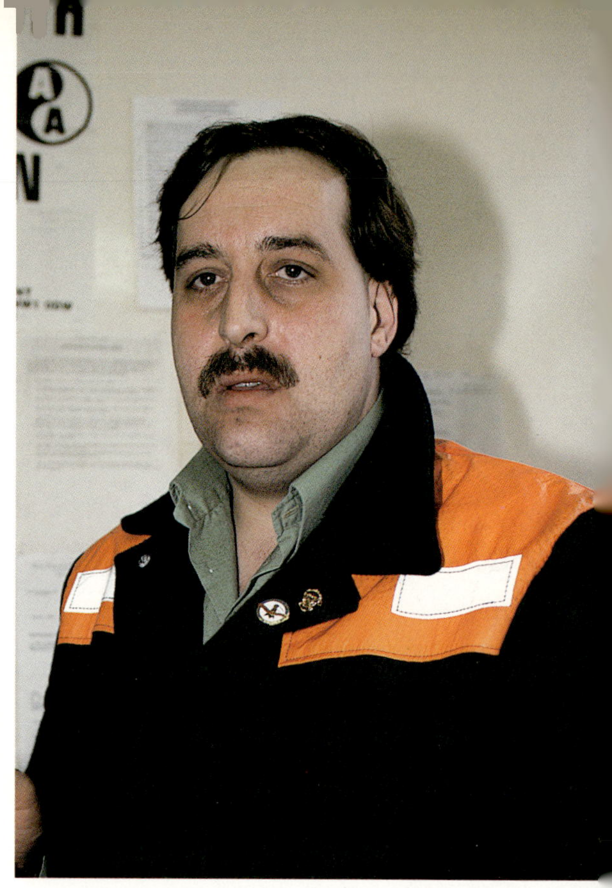
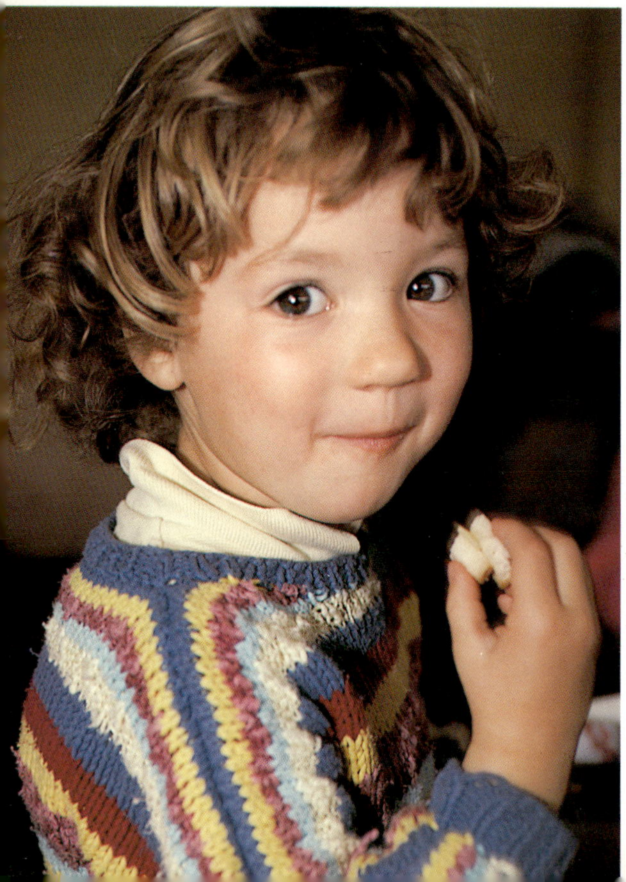
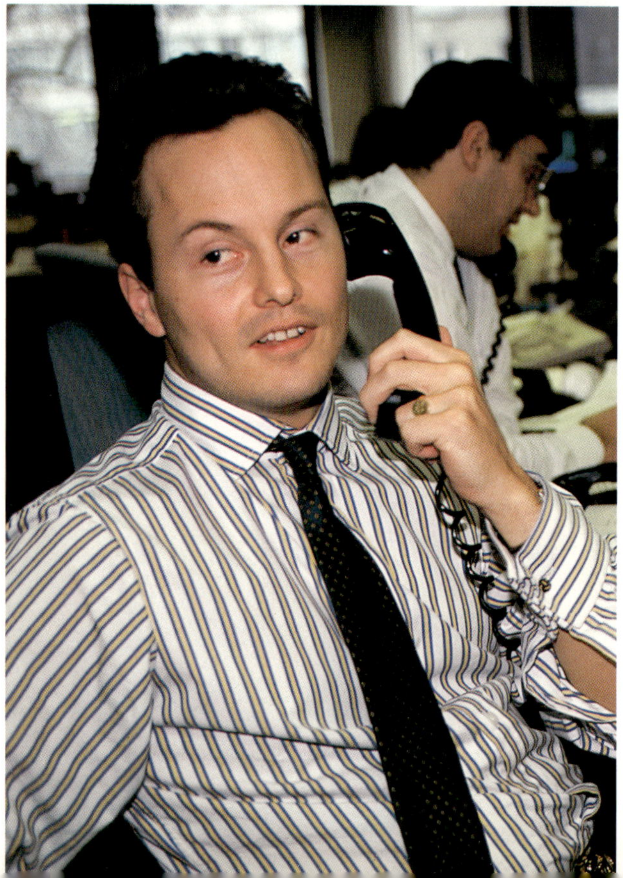
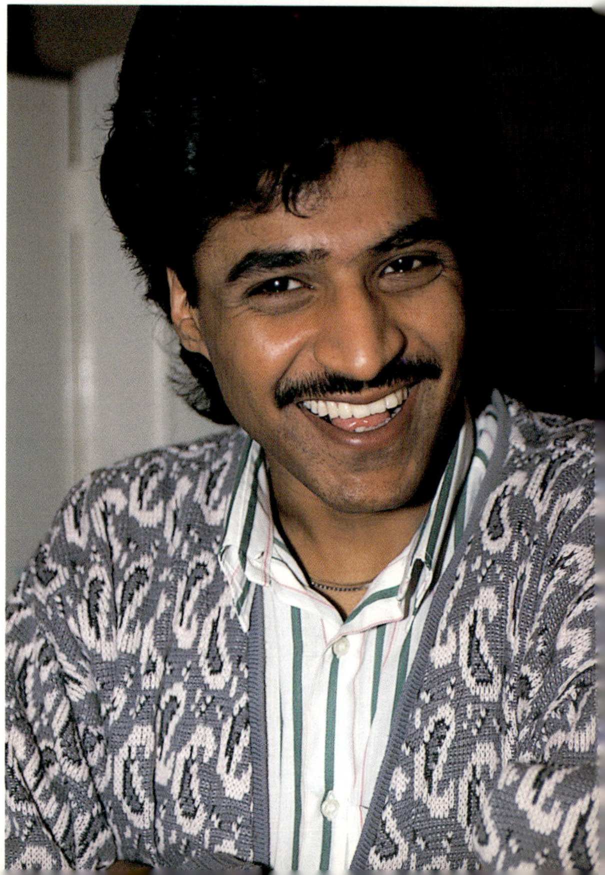

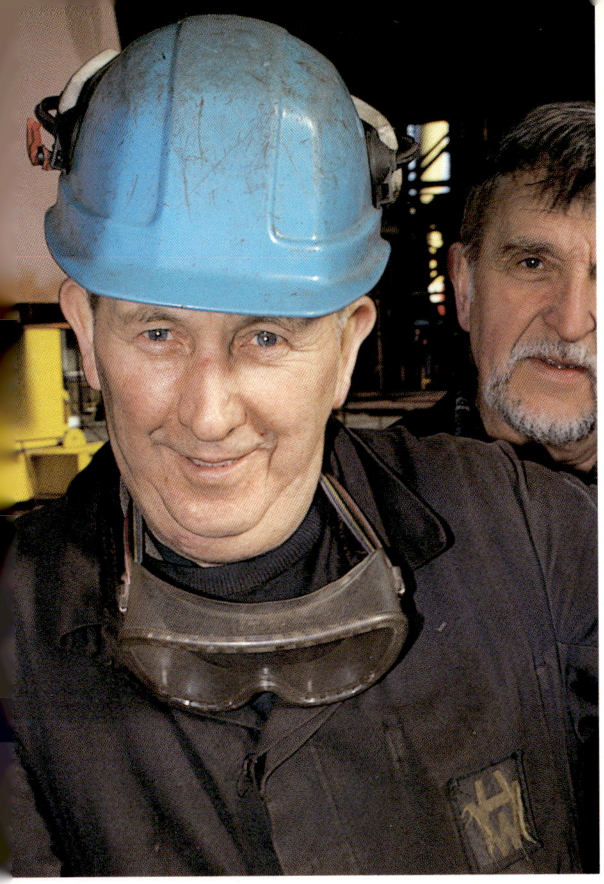
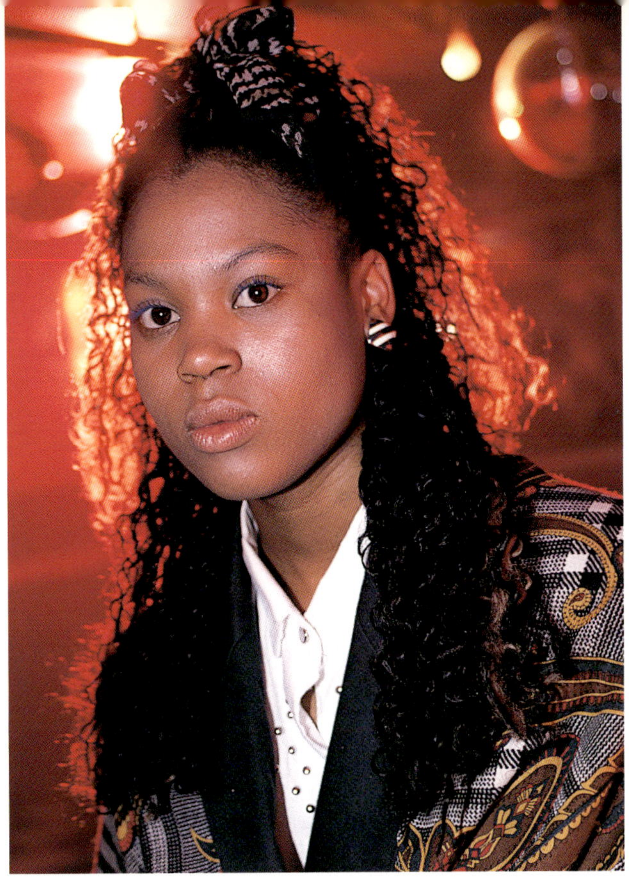
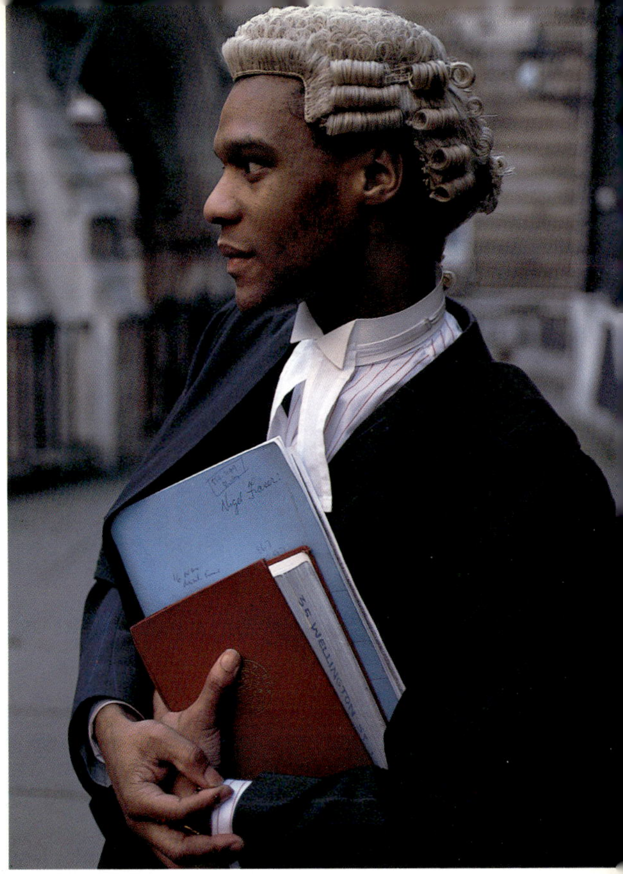
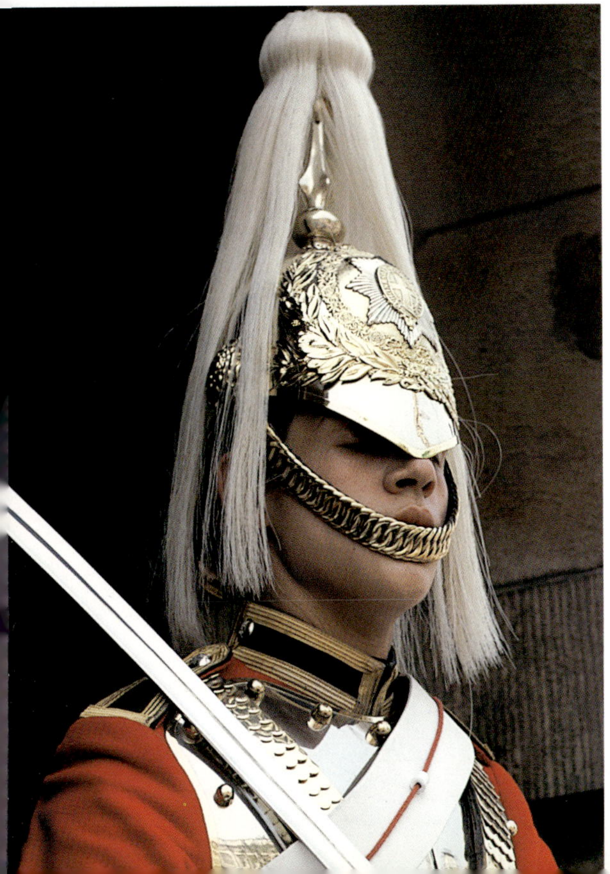
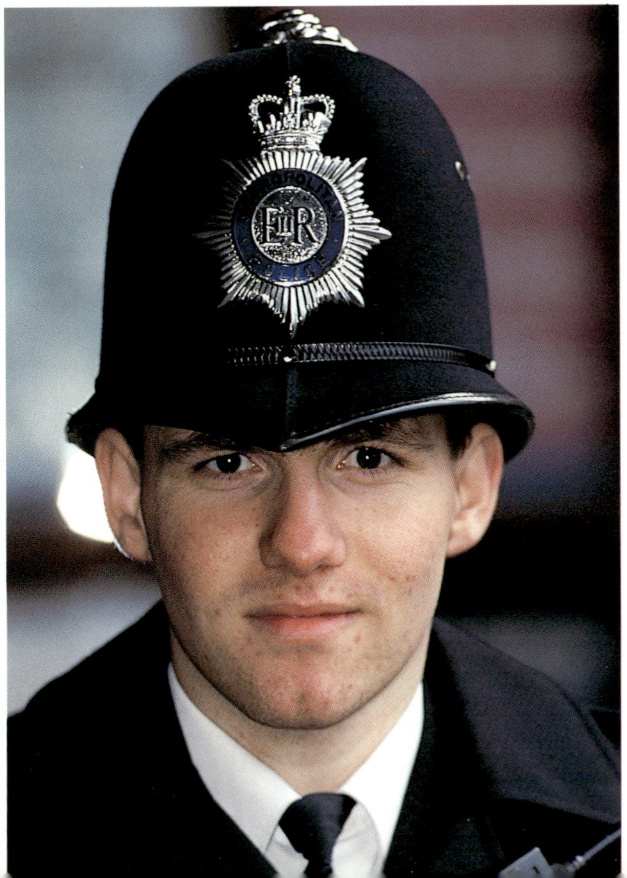
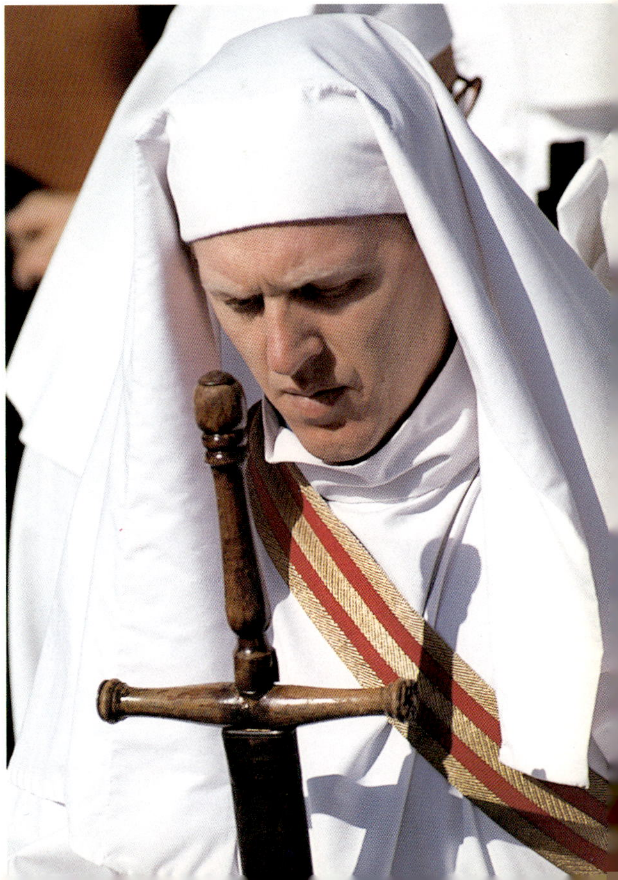

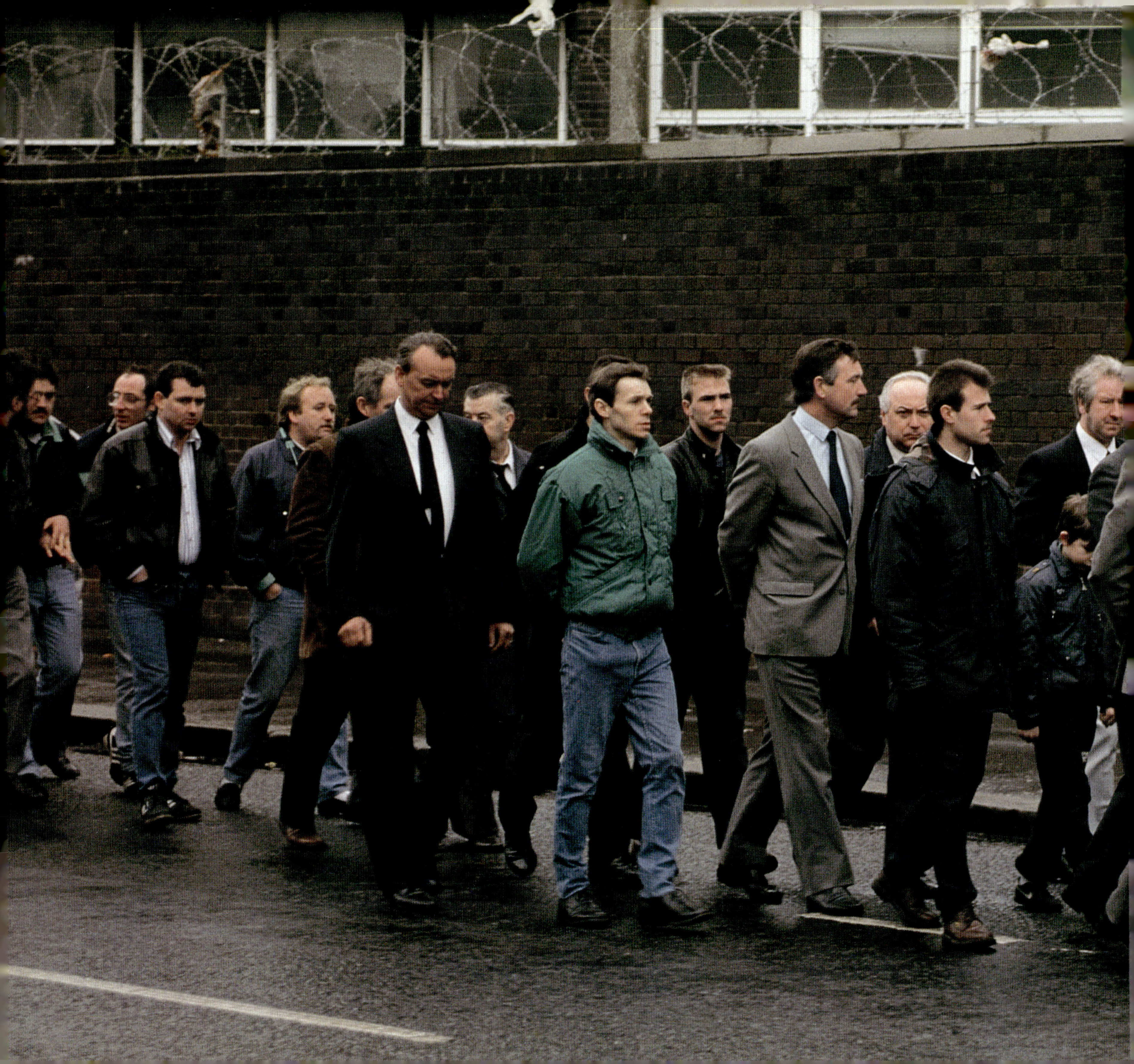

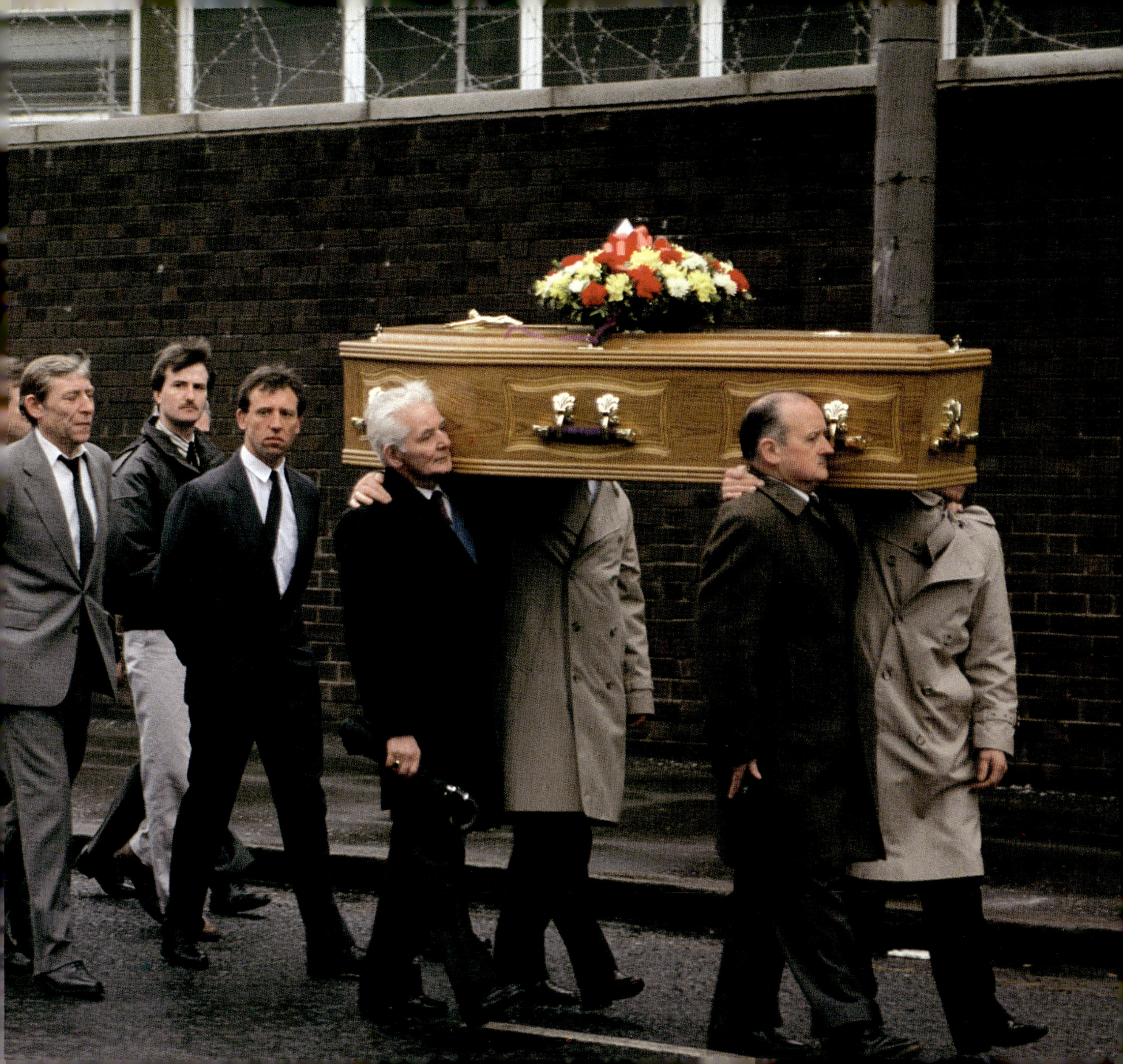

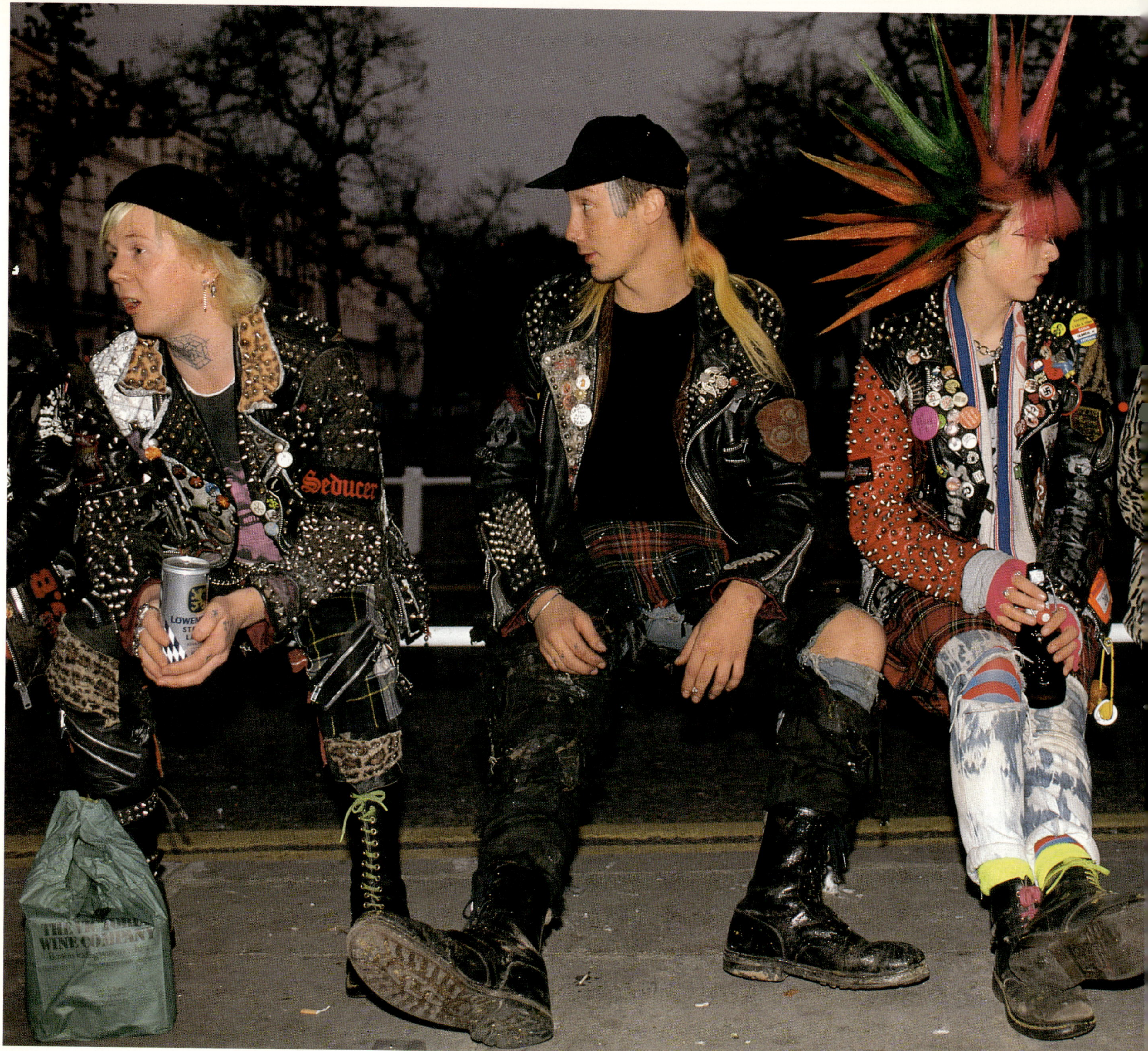
Seducer
WINE COMPANY

PORTRAIT OF GREAT BRITAIN
AND NORTHERN IRELAND

PHOTOGRAPHS BY
MICHAEL REAGAN

EDITED BY LINDA SUNSHINE AND HIRO CLARK

TURNER PUBLISHING, INC.
ATLANTA

To Ira, who maintained a sense of humor long after he should have run out. Without him, this project would not have begun and would surely never have come to fruition.

And to Lena, who taught me a great deal and whose vision and humanity are as much a part of this book as are mine.

Cover: Statue of Winston Churchill, London
Backcover: Forth River, Scotland
Pages 2–3: Easington teenagers
Pages 4–7: Faces of Great Britain and Northern Ireland
Pages 8–9: Funeral procession in the Republican (Catholic) area of West Belfast, Northern Ireland
Title page: Punkers on King's Road, London

Produced by Welcome Enterprises, Inc.
164 East 95th Street
New York, N.Y. 10128

PROJECT DIRECTOR: LENA TABORI
ART DIRECTOR: NAI CHANG
EDITORS: LINDA SUNSHINE, HIRO CLARK
CONTRIBUTING EDITORS: LINCOLN PAINE, BRIDGET ANN BENNETT
COPYEDITOR: TIMOTHY GRAY
MAP: SOPHIE KITTREDGE

PUBLISHED BY TURNER PUBLISHING, INC.
A Division of Turner Broadcasting System, Inc.
One CNN Center
Atlanta, Georgia 30348

DISTRIBUTED BY ANDREWS AND MCMEEL
4900 Main Street
Kansas City, Missouri 64112

Copyright © 1990 Welcome Enterprises, Inc.
Text copyright © 1990 Turner Publishing, Inc.
Photographs copyright © 1990 TBS Productions, Inc.

All rights reserved. No part of the contents of this book may be reproduced by any means without the written consent of the Publishers.

First Edition

Printed and Bound in Japan
1 2 3 4 5 6 7 8 9 10
ISBN 0-8362-6213-1

Contents

INTRODUCTION 15

GREAT BRITAIN 17

STONEHENGE 19

LAND'S END 26

CORNWALL 28

WALES 35

BATH 52

EDUCATION 59
- OXBRIDGE 63
- WINCHESTER 65
- BIRMINGHAM 71

LONDON 74
- POMP AND CEREMONY 76
- THEATER 80
- SIGNS 84
- HYDE PARK 91

Commonwealth   100

Beaulieu   104

The Valley Gardens   108

Cotswolds and Yorkshire   112

Easington   131

Scotland   139
    Glencoe   152
    Isle of Lewis   154
    Standing Stones of Callanish   158
    Foula   161

Northern Ireland   167
    Shipyards   172
    Belfast   174
    Mill Strand Primary School   186

    Acknowledgments   191

Introduction

The story of Great Britain begins in the wild, unwilling sea. Sheared off from Europe by a glacier a quarter billion years ago, the land became a fixed point that ancient cartographers placed "at the top of the world." Innumerable voyagers set foot on its shores, including the Scottis, the Gaels, the legions of Rome, the Angles, Saxons and Jutes, the Vikings, and the Normans—tribes which spoke different languages and together spun a web of myth and legend that settled over the land. In the turbulence, a nation was born.

First and foremost, the people of Great Britain are islanders—isolated and protected, alone and insular. Repeated invasions over the course of a thousand years helped create a particularly British suspicion of outsiders, while the presence of a sea-coast within seventy miles of any spot in Britain strengthened a conception of itself as a separate and unique country.

It was, however, a country destined to expand beyond its own meager borders in the search for resources, trade, cheap labor, and expanding markets. At the same time, the British sought to introduce to the various countries it conquered its own political, religious and moral beliefs. It was a tidal wave of influence that was to have a lasting effect on the world.

The British have always been determined to make a virtue of their separateness by imbuing it with a sense of pride. Today this pride must adapt itself to the needs of a nation in transformation. Having been reduced to its own island frontiers, this once-great Empire is now looking inward to its cities, towns, and streets where a multitude of its former subjects—Asians, Africans, West Indians—inspired by a faith in their own Britishness, have come to claim prosperity. The Empire is no longer to be found overseas—it is being rediscovered at home.

Portrait of Great Britain and Northern Ireland explores the many faces and voices that make Britain what it is today—a nation as firmly fixed in tradition as the rock upon which it rests, and, at the same time, as wild and changing as the enveloping sea.

Come, listen to the voices and see the images of a glorious nation as it struggles to adapt to a changing world, to absorb within its shrunken borders millions of its former subjects, and, ultimately, to fulfill its sea-shrouded destiny.

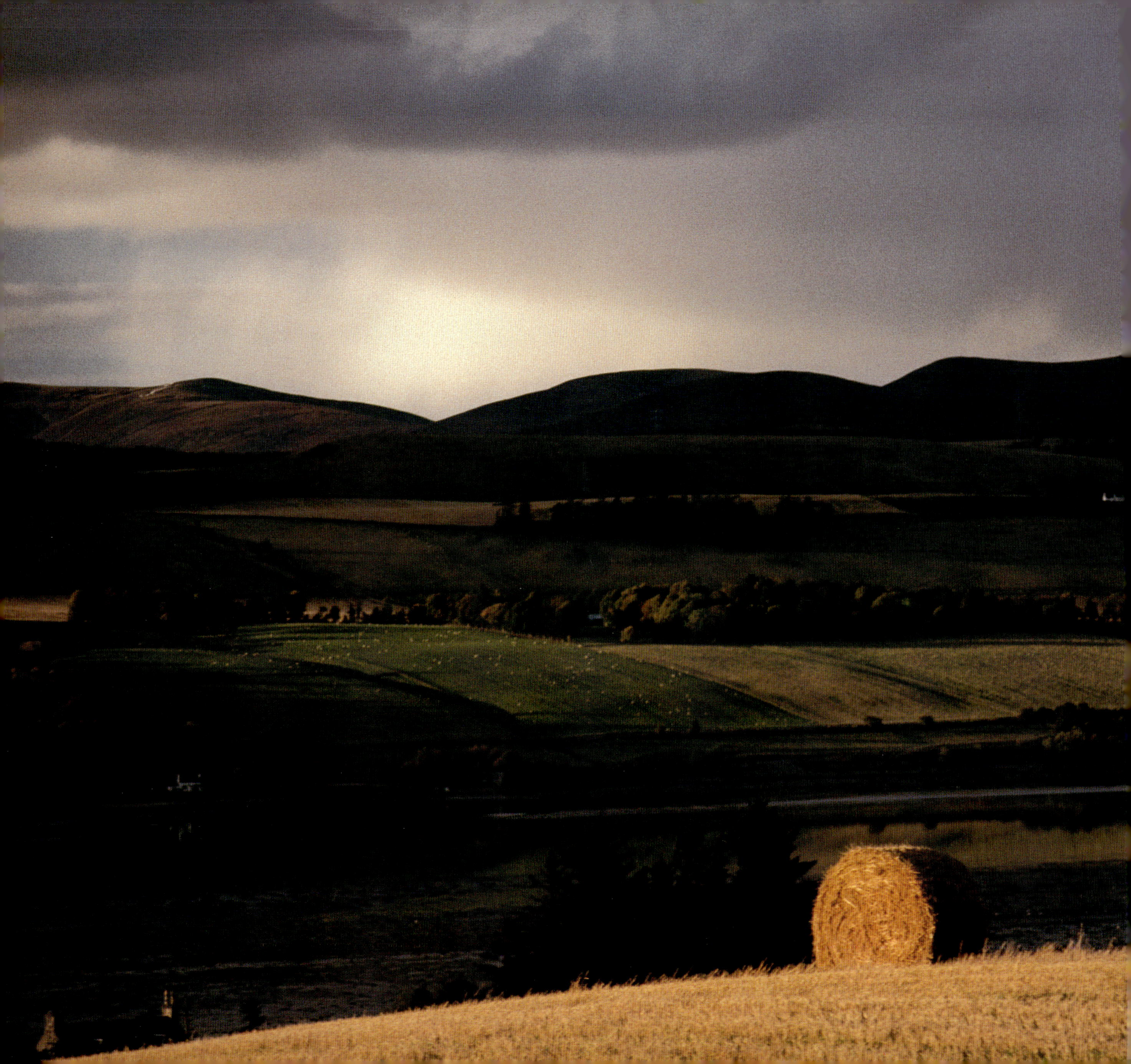

GREAT BRITAIN

Stirling, near the Forth River, Scotland

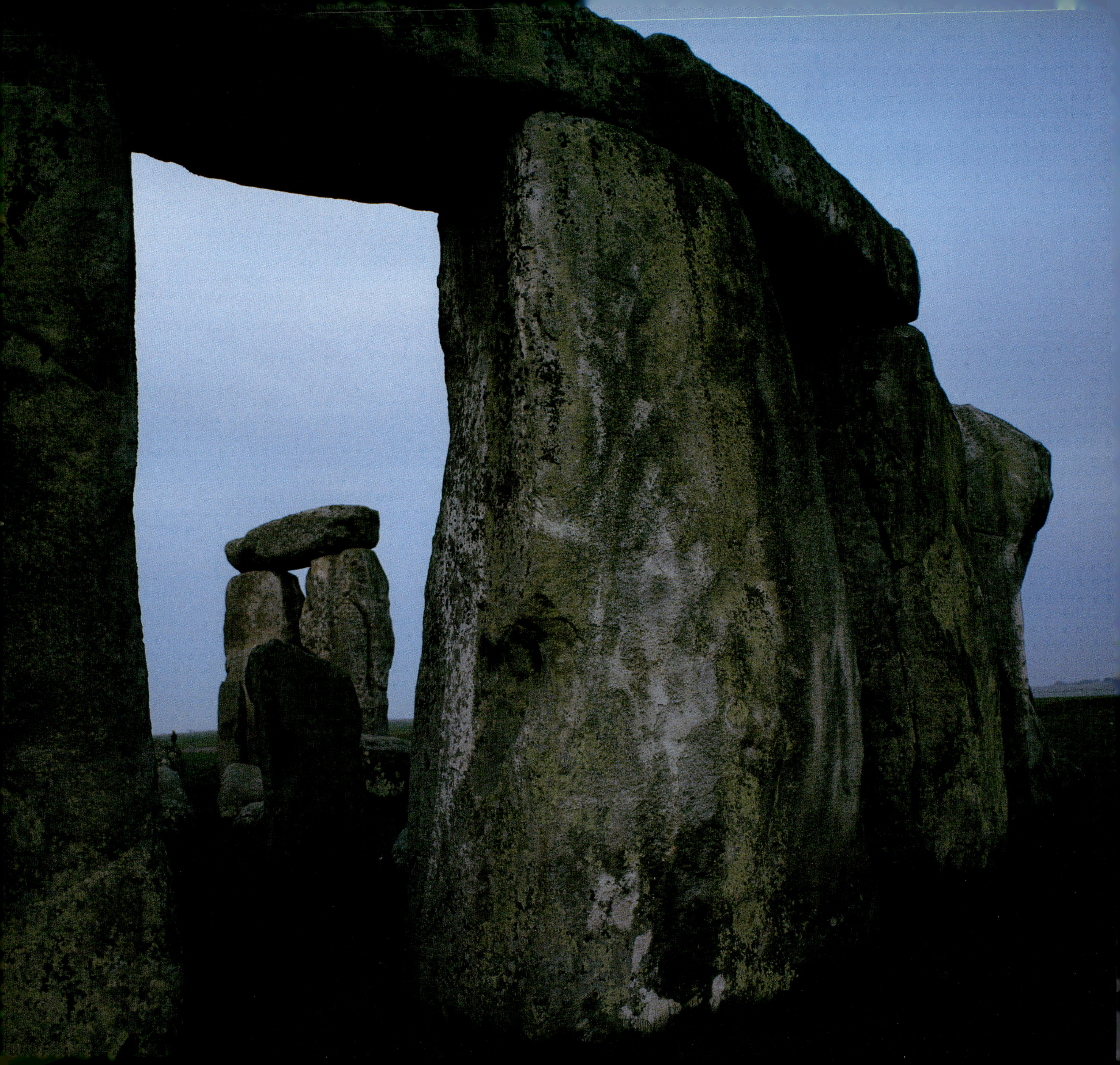

Stonehenge

I saw Eternity the other night
Like a great Ring of pure and endless light,
  All calm, as it was bright,
And round beneath it, Time, in hours, days, years
  Driven by the spheres
Like a vast shadow moved, in which the world
  And all her train were hurled.

—HENRY VAUGHAN (1621–1695),
THE WORLD

The practice of erecting megaliths, or standing stones of great size, grew out of ancient burial traditions and was connected to a sophisticated worship of the sun, moon, and planets. These forms, dating from as early as 3200 B.C., are to be found throughout England and Ireland—and in France from an even earlier time. Perhaps the best known group of megaliths is Stonehenge, found on the Salisbury Plain in southern England. Like the Great Pyramids of Egypt or the stone heads of Easter Island, Stonehenge is a wonder of prehistoric engineering.

The outstanding feature of Stonehenge is two rings of standing stones, the outermost consisting of some thirty sarsen stones and the inner of various bluestones from Wales. Within these circles are two horseshoe-shaped alignments—again, the outer of sarsen stones and the inner of bluestones. The sarsen stones, some of which weigh as much as eight tons, were dragged overland from Marlborough Downs, some twenty miles to the north. The bluestones, dolomitic rocks found only in the Preseli Mountains of southern Wales 135 miles northwest of the Salisbury Plain, were probably transported most of the way via water, along the Bristol Channel to the River Avon, and overland from there to the Salisbury Avon, which then flows a few miles from Stonehenge to

PAGES 18-25: *Sunrise at Stonehenge*

Richard, a Stonehenge security guard

the English Channel. The entire length of this route is 240 miles.

Stonehenge holds as much fascination for the astronomer as it does for the archaeologist. The alignment of the various stones is dictated by the position of the sun and moon over the horizon at various times during the year. The purpose of Stonehenge appears to be related to the observation of the solstices and equinoxes and thereby to the division of the year into fixed periods, presumably for purposes of worship.

In addition to the solar observations, there are four outer stones against whose alignment the Stonehenge builders could sight the most southerly moon rises and the most northerly moon sets. If diagonals were drawn between these stones, they would intersect the center of Stonehenge. While the complexity of calculation, organization, and transportation are remarkable enough, it is even more astonishing that the whole complex evolved in a coherent fashion over the course of thirteen hundred years. Yet despite the dedication and ability of these people, whoever they were, almost nothing is known of them.

Throughout the centuries, Stonehenge has fallen victim to many different kinds of marauders. Pillars have been smashed and carried away for such uses as footbridges and walls. Tourists have chipped away fragments for souvenirs. For protection, security guards have been hired. One of them, Richard, says, "I've worked at Stonehenge, on and off, for four years. I've lived here for sixteen. I didn't grow up in the area, but the first time I came to Stonehenge was when I actually started working here. Most people in the area don't actually come to the stones unless they bring their visiting relatives up to see them.

"We're doing a job here, but we don't think it's necessary to protect the stones from people who respect them—who just want to have a look, take a picture, or put flowers down. It's the minority who cause us to be up here. And we do our job as we've been told, which means everybody, no matter who, has to stay out.

"We've had quite a few people jump over the fence, and I had to tell them to leave the area. The land is owned by the National Trust, but the actual stones are owned by the English heritage.

"We're not formally trained, but after working up here for a while you learn which are the best ways to move people. The main, easy way is to be polite; if they don't move after the third request, we ask for police assistance. We usually have dogs on duty, and that's a good deterrent. As soon as visitors hear a dog barking or even just see a dog, they usually move pretty quickly.

"The stones don't seem to get cold on cold, dark

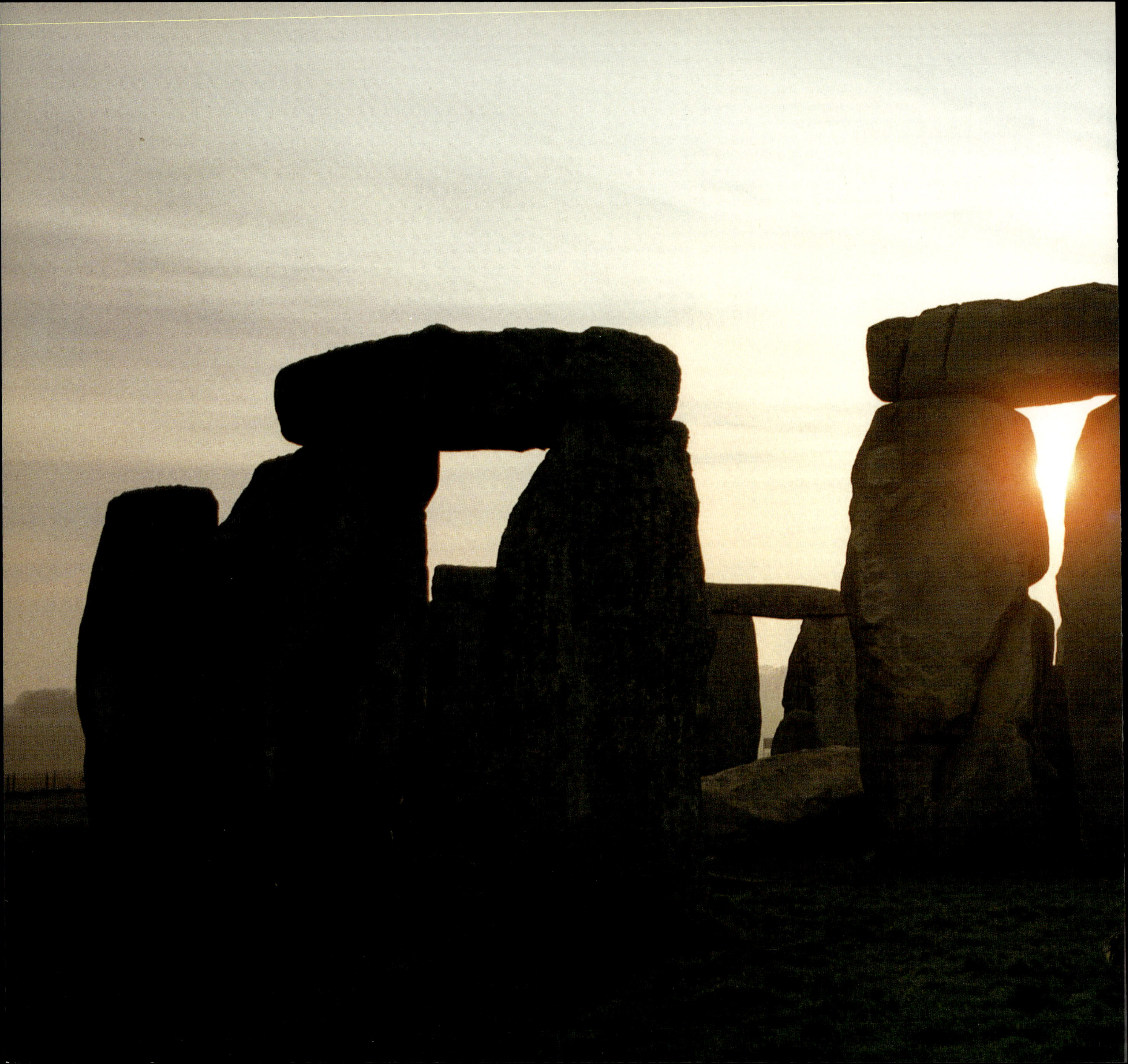

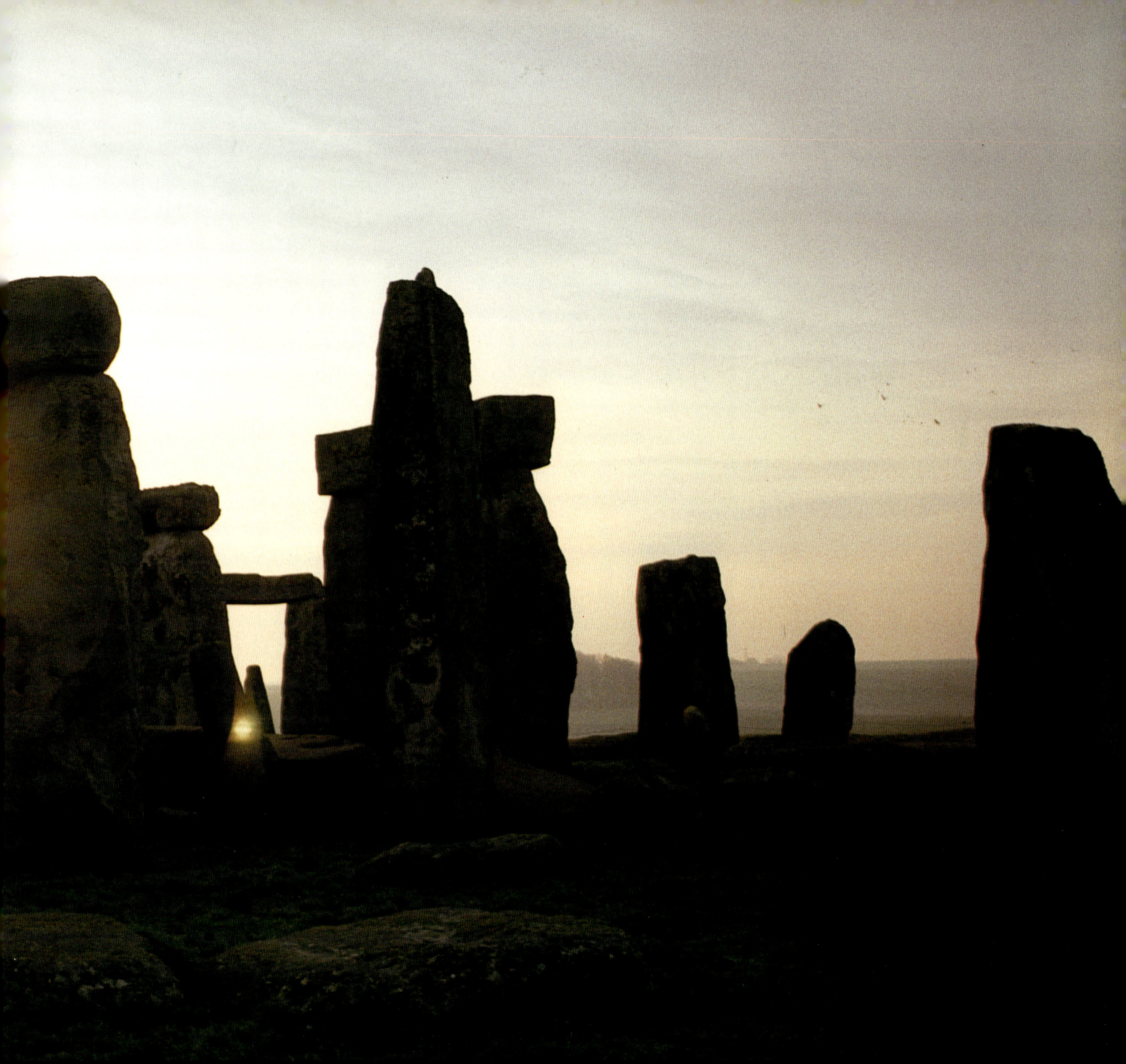

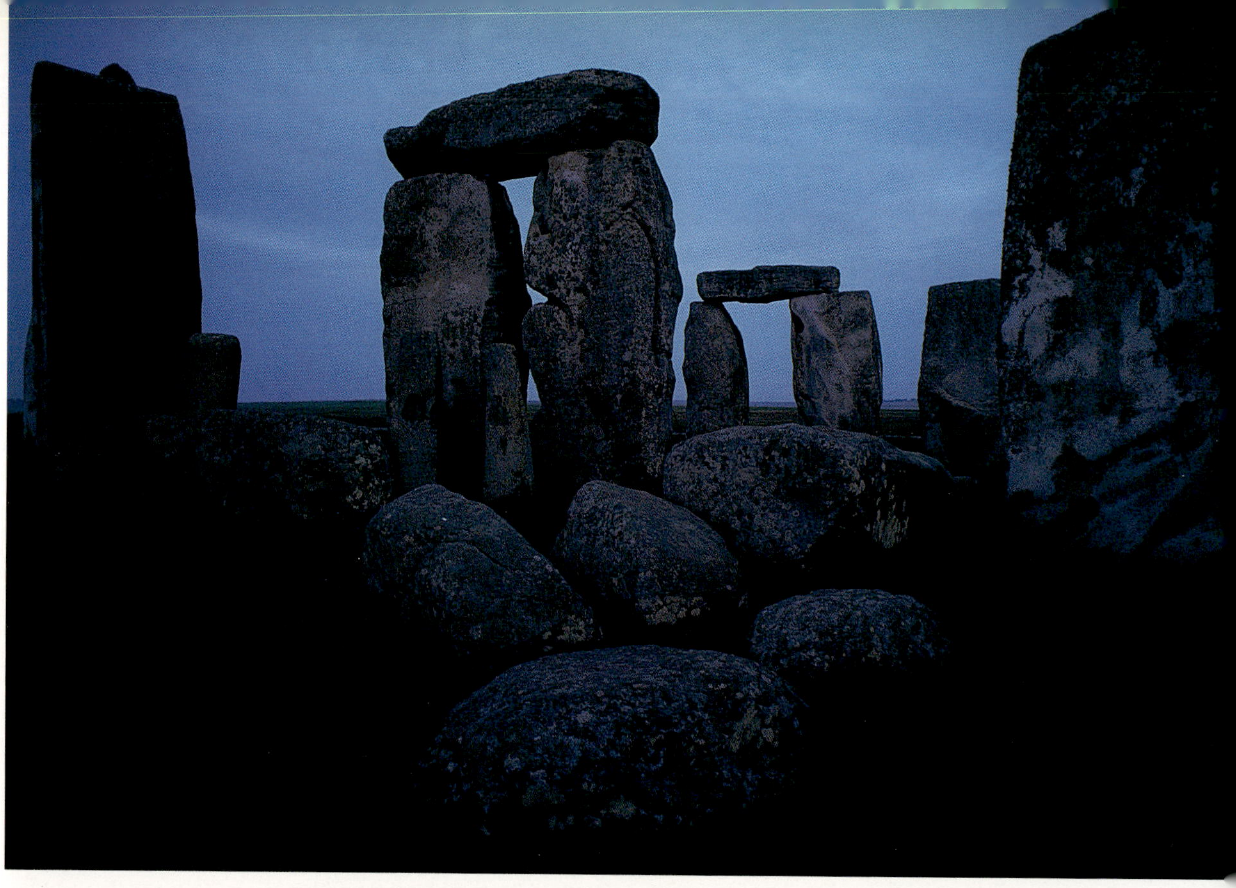

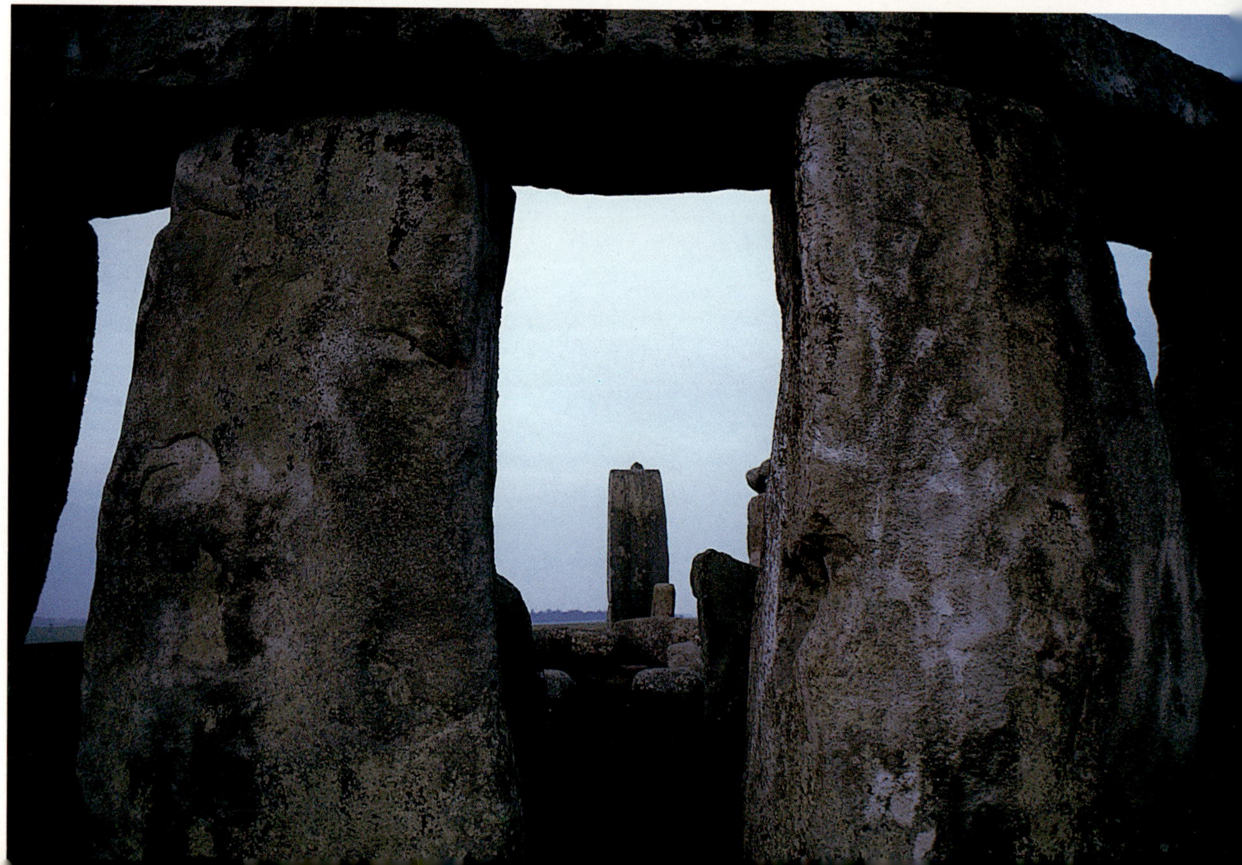

nights. If your hands get really cold, you can touch the stones and actually warm your hands. I wouldn't say that I've actually felt the power. I've had people on the fence—people from America—who have said, 'Can you feel the power?' We try not to look at them too strangely. We say, 'Well, not really.' But maybe that's because we're up here night in and night out."

Land's End

ABOVE AND OPPOSITE: *Land's End, Cornwall*

Cornwall is the southwest extremity of Great Britain, and its rocky point is called Land's End. The people who live in this area are connected to the sea by bonds explained by Englishman James Derham. "My boyhood life was near the sea. My father and his father were both sea captains. They advised me against turning to the sea for a career. But the sea always did fascinate me, and there was always the thought of what was beyond. I mean, you can only see so far over the waves, and what's on the other side of that?

"I had a sense of adventure, especially in those days when I was at school. Half of the atlas seemed to be colored in red, which meant it belonged to the British Empire. It was very intriguing and made me extremely proud to be British. When I was a youth—that's in the twenties and thirties—the British had a very large empire. And this never ceased to amaze me—the fact that a small island could control almost half of the world."

Derham also explains how the smallness of the island profoundly affected its inhabitants. "We became an empire mainly because we're an island. We couldn't produce enough food or anything else to support us, so naturally we had to look elsewhere. We became a great seafaring nation in search of food and raw products to bring back to England. At the same time, we had to protect our returning merchant ships. Therefore, there must have been a tremendous amount of pride in being an explorer, in going out and searching for unknown lands and, in fact, conquering them.

"Psychologically speaking, being an islander makes you want to express yourself, to go somewhere or do something, rather than be enclosed by the shores of the small island on which you live. For this reason, I think, we did produce many explorers—firstly by sea, later by land, and eventually by air."

Farther east of Land's End lies the Cornish port of Plymouth, which has always served as a point of departure to the open sea. It was from Plymouth that Sir Francis Drake embarked on his around-the-world voyage in the *Golden Hind* in 1577. Nine years later, he again set out from Plymouth to intercept and rout the Spanish Armada. Plymouth is also the point from which the Pilgrims sailed in 1620 on the last leg of their perilous voyage to the New World. In fact, it is from this place that the islanders have always set out, staking their fortunes and risking their lives on the vagaries of the sea.

Cornwall

In past centuries, inhabitants along Cornwall's treacherous coastline occasionally supplemented their incomes by wrecking—that is, erecting false lights to lure ships to their ruin on the rocky shores. Times have changed, and today the men and women often make great sacrifices to save those they would once betray.

The most conspicuous life-saving efforts are carried out under the aegis of the Royal National Lifeboat Institute. Founded in 1824, the RNLI has more than 250 lifeboat stations scattered around the coasts of the United Kingdom and Northern Ireland. They rescue more than a thousand people every year. The courage—there is no other word for it—that the volunteers who man these boats display is beyond question, and all too often they give their own lives in order to save others.

One of the most poignant tragedies of recent years was the loss of a lifeboat and its crew of eight in the failed attempt to rescue the *Union Star* as it floundered in perilous seas during the week before Christmas in 1981. The spirit and bravery of the RNLI is exemplified in author Nigel Calder's account of the loss of the Penlee lifeboat, just around Land's End from Sennan Cove, where the accompanying photographs were taken.

On Penlee Point, behind the Low Lee Rock, a slipway runs down to the water from the red door of a lifeboat house. On a Saturday night, December 19, 1981, the door opened and the lifeboat *Solomon Browne* slid into the raging waters of Mount's Bay. Her eight-man crew came from the picture-book fishing village of Mousehole, guarded by a craggy island just south of Penlee Point. One crew member, Charlie Greenhaugh, was a pub owner who had ceremoniously switched on Mousehole's Christmas lights two days before.

This was the worst night that anyone could remember, and as Coxswain Trevelyan Richards steered past the village, the lifeboat pitched in mountainous waves. The darkness and driving rain made it hard to see anything and *Solomon Browne*'s crew were all too aware of the granite presence that starts beyond Mousehole.

Last house on Land's End

OPPOSITE: *Sennan Cove, Cornwall*

*From *The English Channel* by Nigel Calder © 1986 by Nigel Calder
Reprinted by permission of Viking Penguin, a division of Penguin Books USA Inc.

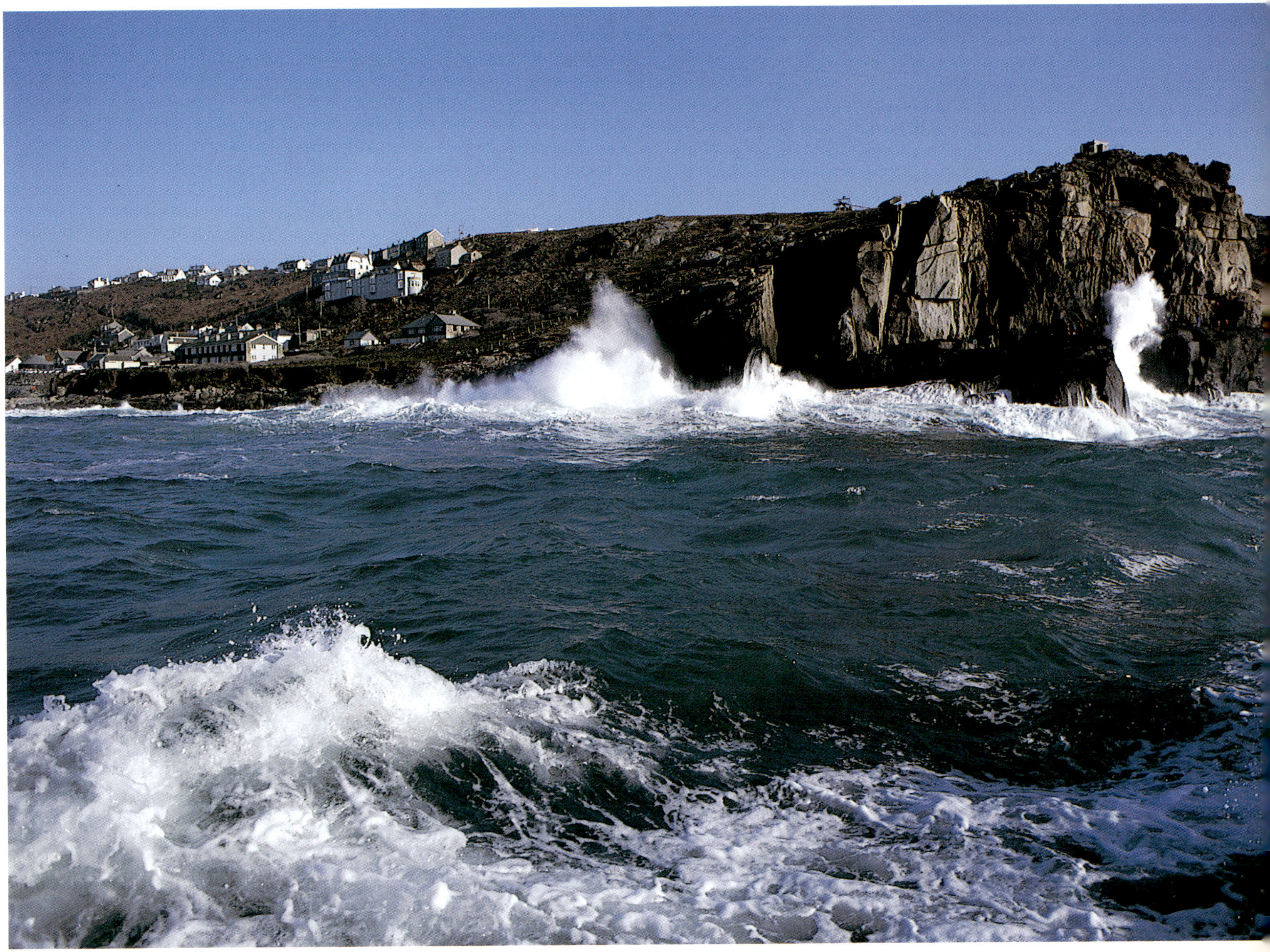

The Dutch captain of an Irish coaster, *Union Star*, had reported engine failure in the Channel some six miles offshore. A storm-force wind gusting to ninety knots [137 miles per hour] was blowing from the south and driving the disabled ship towards this last segment of the English coast. In addition to a crew of four, the captain had his wife and two teenage stepdaughters aboard. The waves tossed the 1400-ton ship like a matchstick, as she drifted close to the Cornish shore.

The peninsula of Penwith, the Celtic name for Land's End, is one of the granite domes that characterize the West Country. The blocky cliffs are terraced and heavy with vegetation, and Carn-du, the next headland, carries pine trees and a pinnacle of rock. A mile farther on, a neat modern lighthouse on Tater-du glints in the morning light. This was where *Solomon Browne* and *Union Star* came to their fatal rendezvous, with Tater-du's flashes, three every fifteen seconds, lighting the wild night like a strobe. The low cliffs have a fringe of shallows and granite rubble around them. A British naval helicopter from Culdrose, piloted by Russell Smith of the U.S. Navy, tried repeatedly to rescue the people aboard *Union Star*, but the weather made it impossible. The ship was close to the shore near Tater-du by the time the lifeboat reached her.

As Coxswain Richards tried to manoeuvre alongside, a huge wave lifted the lifeboat and smashed her down on the coaster's deck. The boat slithered back into the sea. At another attempt, the same thing happened again. Still the lifeboat did not give up. She went in once more, and slammed hard against *Union Star*'s side. This visit gave four of the coaster's peo-

Maurice Hutchens, coxswain of Sennan Cove lifeboat, Royal National Lifeboat Institute. "A man must have no fear of the sea—only respect."

PAGES 30, 31: *A practice launch of the Sennan Cove lifeboat*

30

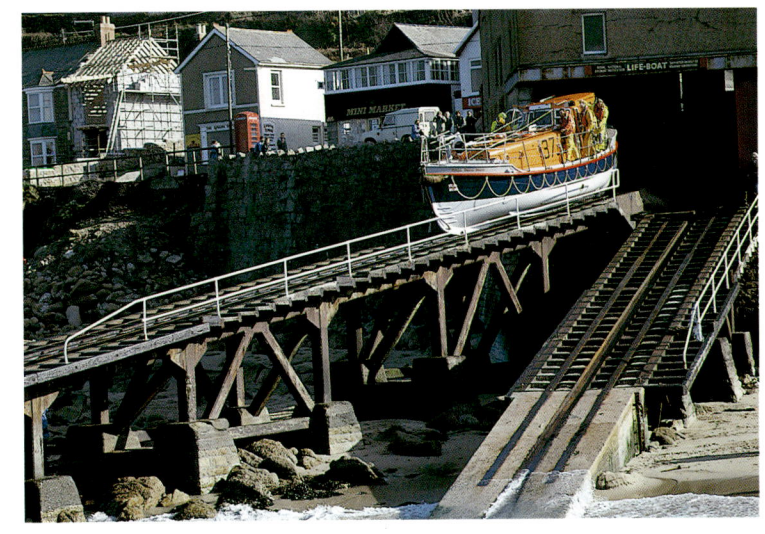

ple the chance to jump aboard the lifeboat. It was already a gold-medal rescue, but there were still four others aboard the coaster, and the rocky shore was only fifty meters away. When last seen, the lifeboat was turning as if for another attempt. A wave overwhelmed the coaster and pitched her on the shore. The lights of the lifeboat disappeared. Victims and rescuers died together in the frenzied sea.

Daylight found *Union Star* upside down at the foot of the cliffs west of Tater-du. Lifeboats from Lizard and Scilly and many local fishing boats were searching the area. Mousehole was already in mourning, but one of the widows told the bishop of Truro, "My husband warned me three weeks ago that this might happen, and that if it did I was not to make a fuss."

Another lifeboat was sent at once to Newlyn to provide temporary cover in Mount's Bay, while fresh volunteers from Mousehole began immediate training for the lifeboat that very soon replaced *Solomon Browne*. Charlie Greenhaugh's Christmas lights were switched on again in Mousehole.

31

St. Michael's Mount, at the center of Mount's Bay, was formerly a bustling port for international trade known as Ictis. The island was given to the monks of Mont. St. Michel in France who established it as a Benedictine priory in the 12th Century. After the Restoration it passed into private hands and is now open to the public.

Glastonbury Tor, a steep conical hill rising up from the flat Somerset plain and all that remains of the 15th Century St. Michael's Church

OVERLEAF: *Lleyn Peninsula, Wales*

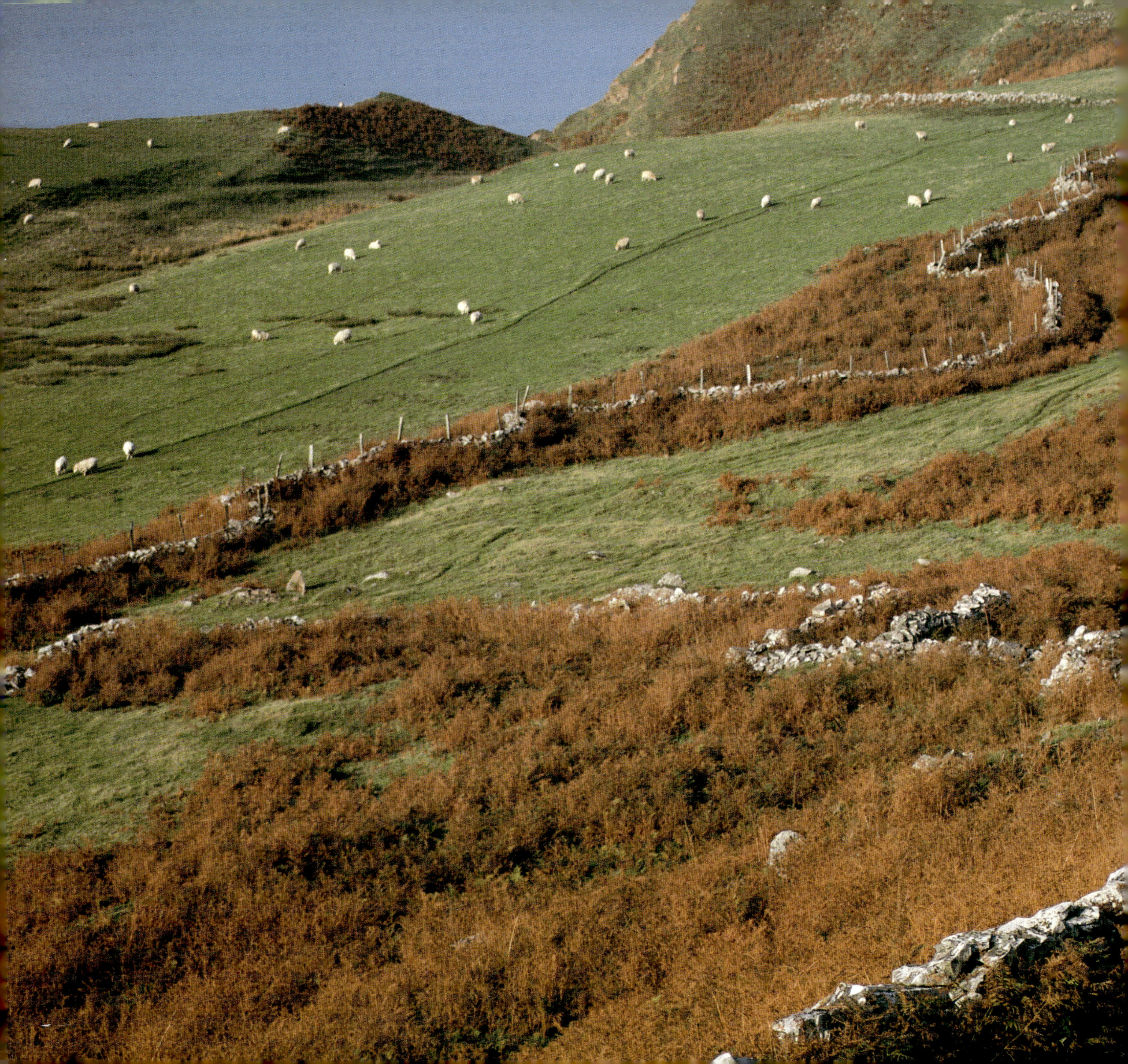

Wales

"It comes as a shock to some people outside Britain, and even within Britain, that so many people in Wales regard themselves as belonging to a completely different nation. The Welsh character is quite different from the English character, although we do feel more of an affinity with the people to the north of England than with those in the south. There's a historic link there because the Celts, as they came from Europe across to Britain, finally settled in the northern and western peripheries. And, of course, we are one of the Celtic nations. And the Welsh language is one of the Celtic languages."

This sentiment, expressed by Welsh nationalist singer Daffyd Iwan, is by no means unique, and its accuracy is certainly confirmed by historical fact. "Most historians," Iwan continues, "agree that there was a Welsh nation emergent in 383 A.D., when Magnus Maximus, the Roman general, left Wales and was recalled to Rome. Left to its own devices, Wales was more or less an independent, Welsh-speaking nation. So that's sixteen hundred years we've been here. Along the way, we've been integrated into England, and we've been exploited, too. We have quarreled amongst ourselves almost all of the time, but we are still here. And Wales is still going."

Wales is attached to the British mainland but separated from it, partly by the sea and partly by a spine of mountains. This division has helped preserve the Welsh identity against outside influence. Despite the encroachment of English authority over the centuries, there has been little assimilation of English ways until recently. "The mountains have been very central to everything," Iwan explains. "The mountains became a sort of fortress and made it difficult for the outside world to reach and influence us. When the Bible was translated into Welsh and the chapels used the Bible as a means of teaching people to read, write, and become centers of community life, the

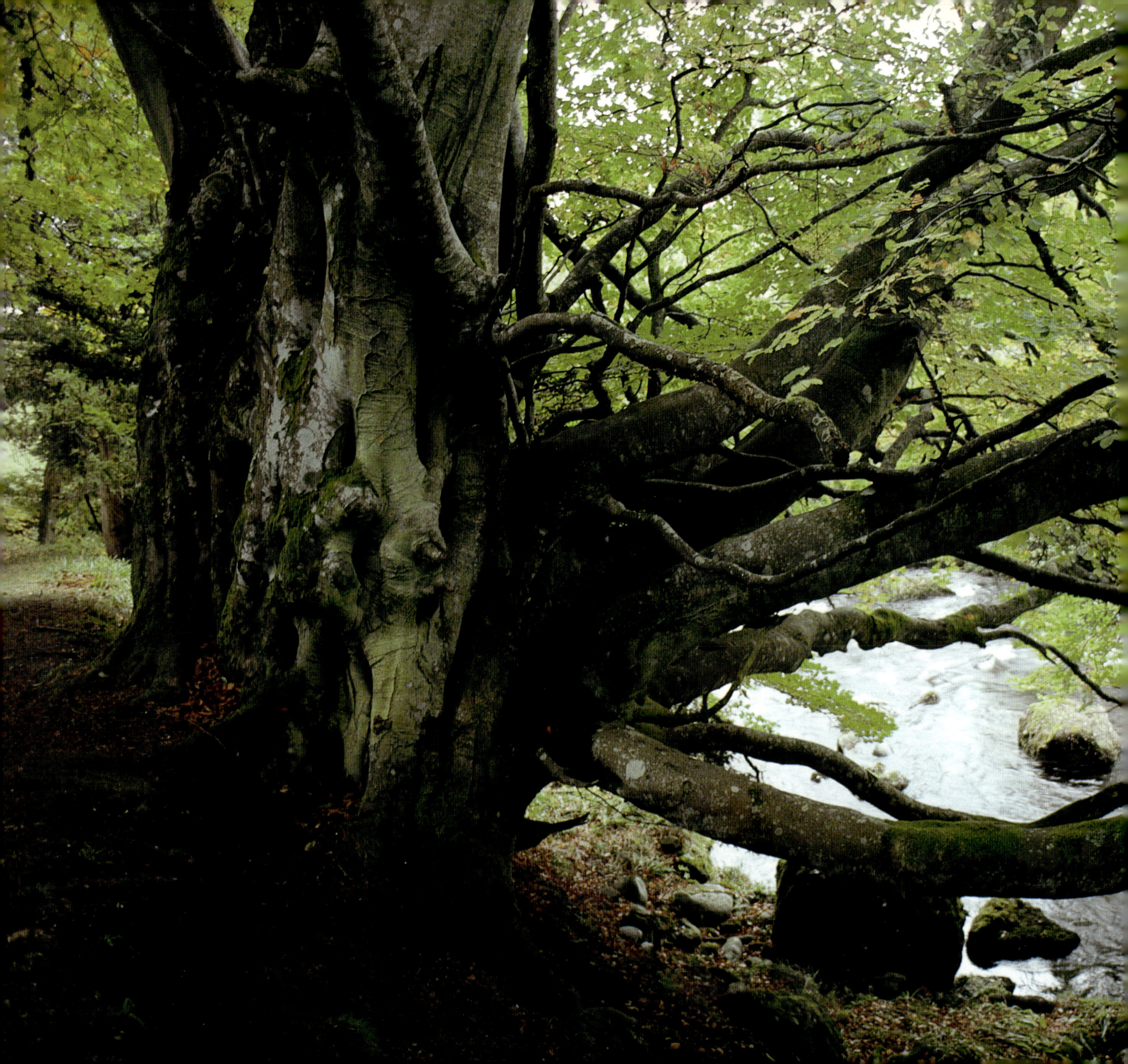

Trees are regarded with particular veneration in the Druidic tradition. Druids, an ancient order of priests in pre-Roman Britain, performed their rites in oak groves and practiced divination, astrology, the art of healing, and suggestive magic.

Near Nefyn, Lleyn Peninsula, Wales

OPPOSITE TOP: *Aberdaron, Lleyn Peninsula, Wales*

OPPOSITE BOTTOM: *Near Caernarfon, in northern Wales*

Welsh language became the spoken, written, and read language of the whole nation. The mountains protected us from too much intrusion. Of course, mass media—television and so on—has changed all that."

In the 1970s, there was a resurgence of Welsh nationalism, the most pronounced manifestation being the attempt to revive the dying language. Welsh, along with Breton, Irish, and Scottish, is one of the four extant Celtic languages. Iwan, a champion of the ancient tongue and the Golden Age of Wales, is an embodiment of this rebellion:

"My whole life revolves around the Welsh language—my songs, my personal life... everything is done through the Welsh language. A lot of people would say that the Welsh tend to be romantics and have their heads in the Celtic mist. Poetry and song is a natural medium for Welsh people.

"There is far more color and imagination in the Welsh character than there is in the English character. Poetry and song and romance come easier to the Welsh character than to the English. And Ireland, of course, is very similar to us. We like to use words, we like to play around with words. We have produced and we are still producing great poets. In Welsh culture, there is still a great emphasis on poetry."

Indeed, the Welsh language boasts one of the oldest literary traditions in Western Europe. The earliest surviving native literature in the British Isles includes the *Mabinogion*, a collection of tales from Celtic mythology that was once universally appreciated in Britain. What distinguishes it from other ancient literatures are fantastic impressions of nature and the mutability of the physical world, expressed especially in the ease with which gods and humans change their forms and in which even plants and animals have dual natures.

"Speaking Welsh," says Iwan, "is a political act in and of itself, because it's declaring, 'We are still here, we are speaking this language which has been spoken on this

39

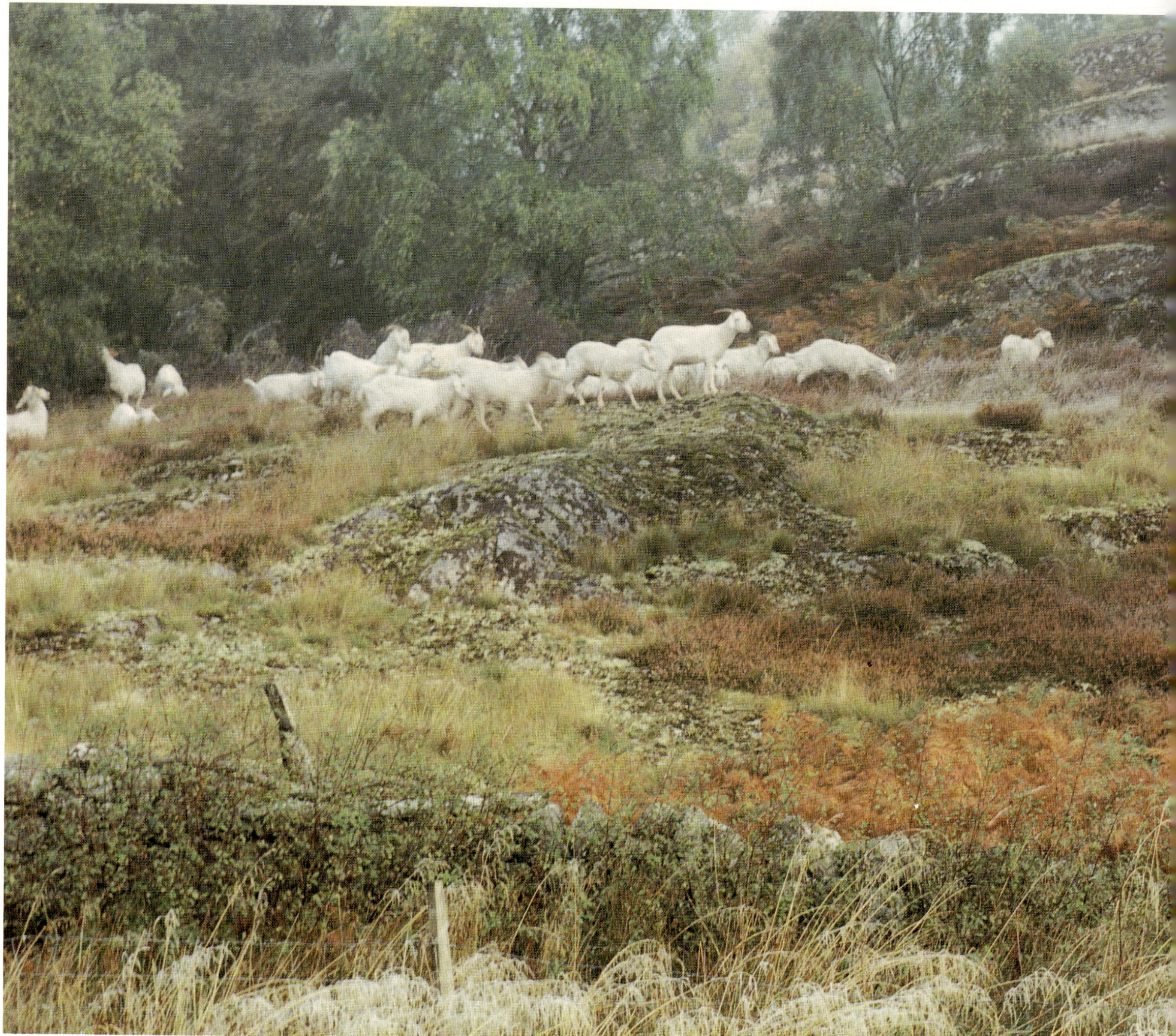

Frosty morning in Wales

Castle in South Wales

piece of land for sixteen hundred years, at least. We are a part of a European culture in our own right.' We want to see ourselves as a European people rather than as a British people. A culture that is lost is like water poured on the earth... you can never get it back."

The earth and the soil are truly the bedrock of Welsh nationalism, and in modern literature the imagery of the land is nowhere richer than in the poetry of David Jones.

In *The Sleeping Lord*, the Anglo-Welsh poet summons the memory of Arthur, Britain's once and future king, and combines a fantastical vision of the land with a deep longing for the roots and meanings, as well as the hopes, of history:

Yet he sleeps on
                      very deep is his slumber:
how long has he been the sleeping lord?
are the clammy ferns
                      his rustling vallance
does the buried rowan
                      ward him from evil, or
does he ward the tanglewood
                      and the denizens of the wood
are the stunted oaks his gnarled guard
                      or are their knarred limbs
strong with his sap?
Do the small black horses
                      grass on the hunch of his shoulders?
are the hills his couch
                      or is he the couchant hills?
Are the slumbering valleys
                      him in slumber
                      are the still undulations
the still limbs of him sleeping?
Is the configuration of the land
                      the furrowed body of the lord
are the scarred ridges
                      his dented greaves
do the trickling gullies
                      yet drain his hog-wounds?
Does the land wait the sleeping lord
                      or is the wasted land
that very lord who sleeps?

Being Welsh is more than simply recalling history and legend. It entails reviving the whole culture that the lan-

Tim Mowday, gardener on the Seiont Manor in Caernarfon, Wales

★From *The Sleeping Lord and Other Fragments* by David Jones
Reprinted by permission of Faber and Faber Ltd.

Slate mine in Wales

Rows of houses with traditional slate roofing, Caernarfon, Wales

Daffyd Iwan, a Welsh nationalist who has gained prominence in the movement to revive the Welsh language. A poet by vocation and an architect by training, he is also a gifted composer and folk singer.

guage represents. "The important thing," says Iwan, "is to draw on the past or carry something from that past to a modern form of being Welsh."

"There are two million people who are Welsh but who don't speak it. Of course the Welsh identity does encompass those as well. If you tell people living in the South Wales valleys—although they don't speak Welsh, they speak English with a very pronounced Welsh accent—if you tell them that they're English, they would certainly correct you and say, 'Good God, no, we're Welsh.' And that means more than just belonging to a region.

"Of course there are outside signs—national institutions like a national library, a national museum, a national folk museum, a national anthem, national rugby and soccer teams, and so on—giving us the trappings of a nation. But the spirit of Wales is something else again. Wherever you go in Wales, there are signs of the past—including the castles built by the Welsh princes to keep the English out and the castles built by the English kings to keep Wales down once they conquered us. But those

Dafydd Ap Tomas, owner of the Plas Glyn-y-Weddw gallery, dedicated to Welsh art and located in Llenbedrog, Wales

45

Caernarfon Castle, the seat of the Prince of Wales and backdrop of the July 1960 Investiture of H.R.H. Prince Charles as Prince of Wales (an office conferred to the male Heir Apparent of England since 1282)

OPPOSITE: *Caernarfon Castle, situated on the Menai Strait, at low tide*

castles are symbolic of our past, and the wonder is that they failed. These castles were built with imported towns around them, actually transplanting people from England into Wales with the purpose of anglicizing the whole area. But around these castles you still find a Welsh-speaking community. It's quite an amazing feat that a nation so close to the center of what became the British Empire has managed to survive.

Great Manson Farm, Monmouth, South Wales

"What is making it very, very difficult at the moment is this constant draining of people from Wales, mainly young people looking for work and leaving Wales to find jobs. At the same time, we have a replenishment of that lost population from the English people who come to live in Wales because they want to get away from the towns and cities. They want to live near the mountains and the sea and the rivers and the solitude of the country, the beautiful cottages. We've got everything they need here, and on top of that, of course, the property in Wales is fairly low-priced. During the last five years, Wales has changed beyond recognition. Some areas have changed from being Welsh-speaking to English-speaking communities.

"Now there is a reaction, and to put it in perspective, I should say that it's happening in rural England as well. The people of the rural areas in England suddenly feel that their way of life is being taken over by English town people and yuppies from the city who've got more money and who come in and buy old properties. Now if that is a problem in rural England, then it's far more of a prob-

Arnold Miles, owner of the Great Manson Farm

49

LEFT AND BELOW: *Lambing season on the Great Manson Farm*

OPPOSITE RIGHT: *Francis and Tommy Brain, cidermakers, live on a farm their family has held for over four generations in the Forest of Dean, Gloucestershire.*

OPPOSITE LEFT: *Tommy was once a prosperous sheep trader.*

lem in Wales, because you also have the differences in nationality and language."

Many Welsh do feel that the relationship between Wales and England has been a colonial one, in which Wales has been exploited and given second-class status by the dominant English. Iwan states, "There are some outstanding examples of English people who've come in here and started a business and provided work. But usually the English are here to run an industry, and if the profit is not there, they leave. This is the classic tale of the exploitation of the coal and slate of Wales. The wages have been very, very low. The price paid was very, very high. There was always a danger of being killed or suffering lung disease. And yet when coal became too expensive to dig out, the whole industry closed down with hardly any compensation."

But, as Iwan insists, "I think the Welsh people must face this challenge and say, 'Look, we're not going to be overrun again. We've got to seize the opportunity.' If a people, if a community, believes that they're about to disappear or are part of the dying, they've got two choices: they can either escape by becoming part of the winning side or descend into total despair. There are signs in Wales and Ireland of despair setting in sometimes. You will meet a lot of people in Wales who will tell you, 'There's no hope, we are fighting a desperate battle that cannot be won.' But I'm not really interested in that. I think there is always a more positive side to things. It's a question of adapting and changing. We have to face the fact that some things will change. We have to face the fact that traditions do end. But out of it, we can create a new beginning and a new form of Wales."

Bath

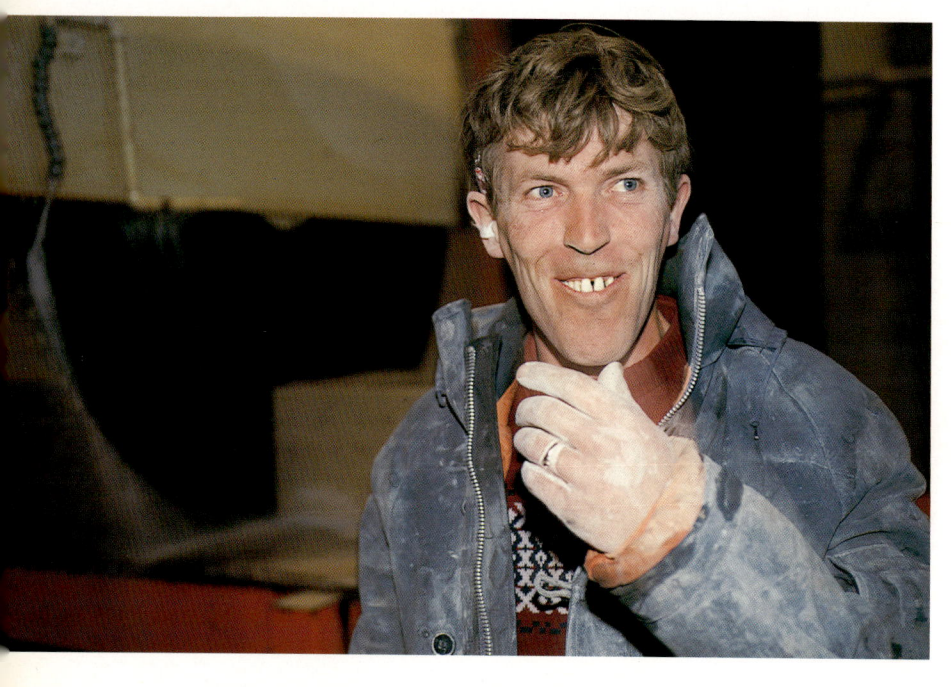

Bath stonecutters

"There's an old-fashioned saying," says third-generation master mason Roger Williams of Bath, "that once you get the stone dust in your lungs, you will always enjoy working with the stone. And if that's the particular line of business you want to go into, and if you train as an apprentice with a good company and can stick to it, then you will always be a stone mason. As I say, once you get the skill, and you get the stone dust in your lungs, you tend to stay a stone mason all your life."

Williams employs thirty-eight men to mine the prized oolitic limestone, known simply as Bath stone. "We get most of the block from places around the Bath area, from Corsham and from a quarry that has reopened at Limpley Stoke, which is a very hard, textured stone. We have to mine it, and when it comes to the surface it hasn't seen the light of day for fifty million years. We put it on our saws and cut it down into smaller blocks, and then it's finished by our masons. When you wander along the street and look up at the mouldings and the cornices, you see the same old stone that's come out of the ground. It's a wonderful feeling."

Among those mouldings and cornices are the ones erected two millennia ago by the Romans, who were attracted to the area not for the architectural possibilities but for the thermal springs from which Bath takes its modern name. The Romans called it *Aquae Sulis*—the waters of Sulis—after an important Celtic deity. Using chiefly the limestone outcroppings of the surrounding area, they built elaborate baths (complete with a pump house) around the open springs and turned the remote provincial town into a popular resort. This gave the city a refinement and sense of style that it enjoys to this day.

Only faint echoes of its former Roman grandeur remain in Bath today, for after the legions had quit Britain, the city fell into a state of neglect and ruin. Even in the Middle Ages the ruins of the ancient city held a special fascination for those who visited, as the following anonymous poem from the eighth century attests:

OVERLEAF: *Roman Bath with Bath Abbey in the background*

THE RUIN

Wondrous this masonry wasted by Fate!
Giant-built battlements shattered and broken
The roofs are in ruin, the towers are wrecked,
The frost-covered bastions battered and fallen.
Rime whitens mortar; the cracking walls
Have sagged and toppled, weakened by Time.
The clasp of earth and the clutch of the grave
Grip the proud builders, long perished and gone,
While a hundred generations have run.
Hoary with lichen and ruddy of hue
This wall has outlasted, unshaken by storm,
Reign after reign; now ravaged and wrecked
The lofty arch is leveled in ruin. . . .
   Firmly the builder laid the foundations,
Cunningly bound them with iron bands;
Stately the palaces, splendid the baths,
Towers and pinnacles pointing on high;
Many a mead-hall rang with their revelry,
Many a court with the clangor of arms,
Till Fate the all-leveling laid them low.
A pestilence rose and corpses were rife,
And death laid hold on the warrior-host.
   Then their bulwarks were broken, their fortresses fell,
The hands to restore them were helpless and still.
Desolate now are the courts, and the dome,
With arches discolored, is stripped of its tiles.
Where of old once the warrior walked in his pride,
Gleamingly with gold and wanton with wine,
Splendidly shining in glittering mail,
The structure lies fallen and scattered in ruin.
Around him he saw a treasure of silver,
Riches of pearl and precious stones,
In a shining city of far-flung sway.
There stood courts of stone, with a gushing spring
Of boiling water in welling floods,
And a wall embosomed in gleaming embrace
The spot where the hot baths burst into air.

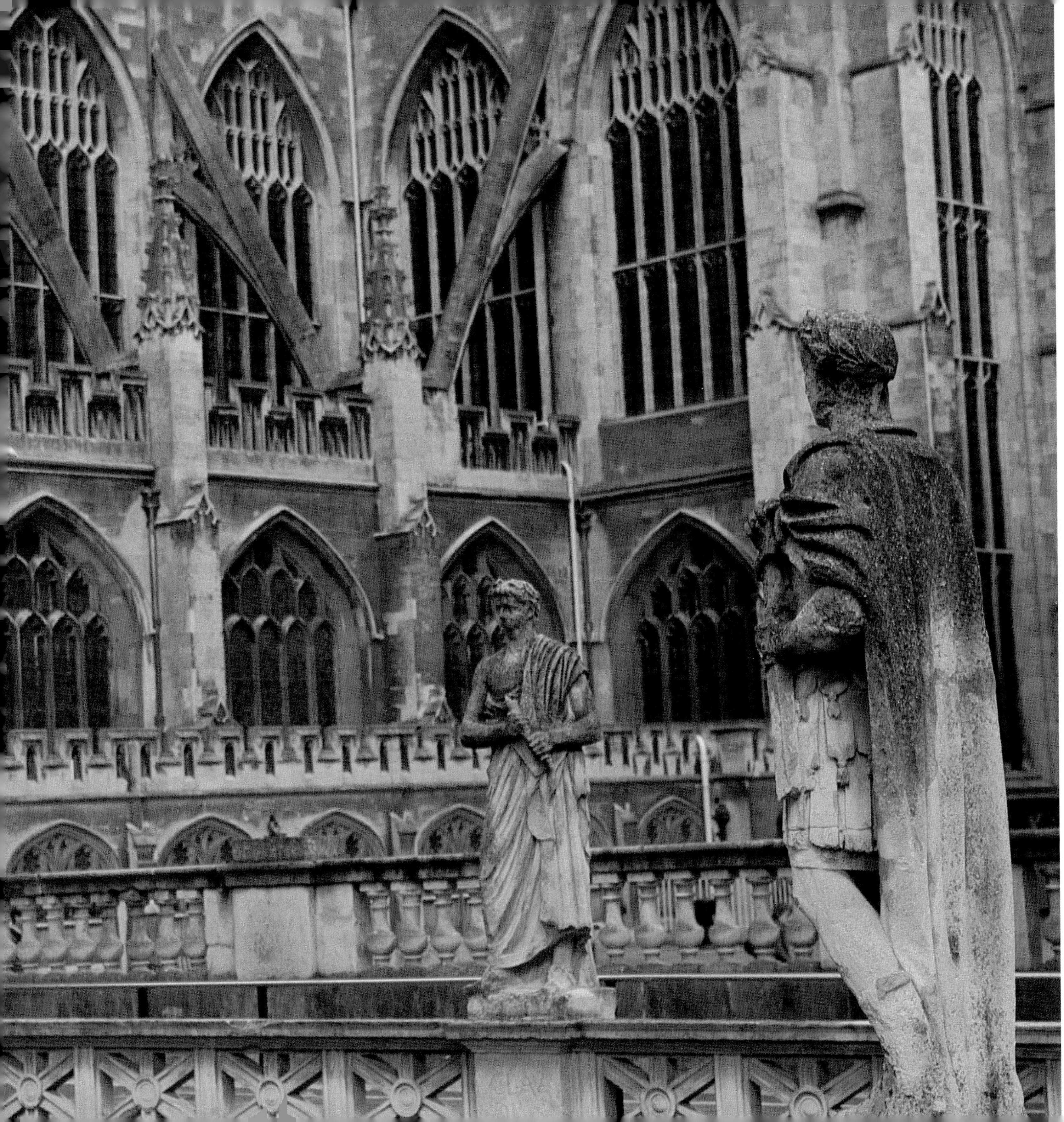

Roman Bath

   This portrait of Bath evokes a sense of longing for a golden, glittering age, but one that reveals more about the time in which the author lived than about the Romans themselves. They are described in terms that would apply more to the Anglo-Saxon warrior kings, and their sudden disappearance is attributed to warfare and disease—calamities which doubtless arose in the wake of their departure but which did not, as we now know, cause their downfall. The physical demise of Bath was not caused only by age and neglect, or even outright warfare, but by the systematic dismantling of the original Roman buildings whose finished stone the Saxons used for new buildings.
   They did not rely solely on the work of their predecessors, however, and starting in the seventh century the stone was quarried in earnest, first for St. Aldhelm's Malmesbury Abbey and in later centuries for other religious structures and private manors. According to the seventeenth-century antiquary John Aubrey, the legend

surrounding the origins of Malmesbury Abbey claimed that while riding by Hazelbury Quarry, "the eminentest free-stone quarry in the West of England," St. Aldhelm "threw down his glove and bade them digge and they should find great treasure, meaning the quarry."

Although contemporary stone cutters use modern machinery with diamond-tipped blades to cut and shape the stone, more ancient methods, dating back hundreds, if not thousands, of years, were employed until quite recent times. Williams recalls the methods of excavating and shaping Bath stone used during his own apprenticeship barely a quarter century ago.

"To get the block out you had what they called a picker, which was a man with a long-handled pick axe. He would get right up into the top part of the seam and get out all of the brush stone on top of the natural Bath stone. He was there all day, picking out this brush stuff and working under terrible conditions—darkness, wetness, in a cramped position—and then the sawyers would go in with the big hand saws, called frig bars, get into the top part that the picker had picked out, and saw down through the blocks. Then, gradually, they would pitch it underneath and lift the block, drill or bash a hole in it with a big chain, and pull the block out from the seam. We would just cut the blocks out of the vast stone and then use the traditional mallet, hammer, and chisel to fashion it into various bits and pieces."

It was not until the eighteenth century that the luxuries of Bath and the quality of its architecture once again matched the Roman achievements. The city's revival as a retreat for the well-to-do began with a visit by Princess Anne in 1692. One man attracted to "the spot where the hot baths burst into air" was the Georgian gambler and dandy Beau Nash, arbiter of taste and Master of Ceremonies for what became, under his inspired direction, England's most fashionable resort. Answering the need for accommodations and amenities suited to the sensibilities of the new upper-class visitors to Bath, the architects John Wood, father and son, designed some of the finest examples of Palladian architecture in Britain, including The Parades, Queen's Square, The Circus, and—Wood the Younger's crowning achievement and the centerpiece of one of Europe's most elegant townscapes—the Royal Crescent.

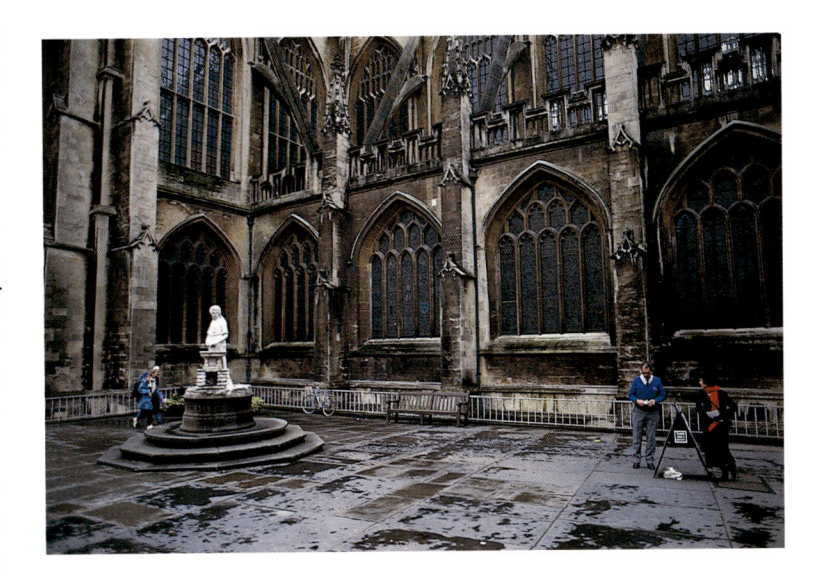

According to Williams, "In this country at the moment, there is a resurgence in the use of natural stone. For a long time, modern architects specified products such as concrete or glass and made use of the modern methods of building, but now they're going back to traditional ways and means. The general public feels that you can't beat natural materials. For example, if you're using wood in a building, then you can't really better that. Builders have tried alternatives—plastic, concrete, and other fabricated materials—but they've come back to the original item."

The revival of stone as a fundamental building material foretells a bright future for Roger Williams and for Bath. "We're very, very busy. We've got a full order book. We took on some additional staff last week, and we'll be taking on some more apprentices shortly. There's a great future in this industry."

*Winchester Cathedral,
Southern England*

Education

At the height of their power throughout the Christian world, churches were closely associated with centers of learning and of the arts, favoring in particular the wealthier classes on whose patronage the Church depended. In England, centers of worship and education, such as Winchester and Christ Church, Oxford, became enclaves of the social elite and remain so today. They are also among the most respected institutions of higher education in Great Britain and, indeed, the world.

While there are now more than forty universities and hundreds of technical colleges in Great Britain, the idea of making education available on a widespread basis is comparatively new and coincides with the rise of a middle class during the industrial revolution. As John Rae, former headmaster of Westminster, explains:

"The great boom in public-school education came in the nineteenth century—post-1830, roughly. That's when every aspiring, up-and-coming family wanted to send their children—boys only at that stage—to a 'public school' [In England public school refers to a private boarding school.] That's when English society became very stratified. Of course, there were classes in eighteenth-century society, as well as snobbery, corruption, and everything that went with it. But because it wasn't fixed rigidly, society was much more fluid. Oddly enough, it was almost easier to make it socially in the eighteenth century by being unscrupulous or brilliant or clever, in some ways even more so than today. It was a much more freewheeling society than the nineteenth century."

Today, in the traditional course, one starts at a preparatory school, succeeds to a public school, and graduates from there to one of the colleges at a university. The competition for entrance to each school stiffens dramatically every step of the way. For those who succeed, it is the beginning not just of an education but of a well connected future.

The educational system for the elite is explained by former prep-school student Andrew Thompson: "I remember when I was about six years old, I went away to a prep school. It was only a small place, but it felt pretty strange to be away from my parents so early in life. I adjusted fairly quickly, because all the kids were in the same boat. When you go to a prep school or a boarding school, it's fairly important to fit in and get on with everybody else, because you won't survive without friends. I think this is the element of all boarding schools that gives kids the strength to keep going.

Choir rehearsal at Hereford. The cathedral's greatest renown, apart from its ecclesiastical functions, is as one of the three cathedrals along with Gloucester and Worcester that hosts the celebrated Three Choirs Festival, one of the oldest music festivals in Europe, dating from the early 18th Century.

"When I was about eleven or twelve, I passed the necessary entrance exams and entered Gordonstoun in Scotland. It's one of our more famous schools. Apart from the great sense of history that we're taught to honor, the schools teach you how to get on with people and control your own thoughts, as well as helping you decide what you want to do and believe in those decisions. The stiff-upper-lip routine, really: If you're right, don't be shy. Go out there and make sure people know you're right. It gives you courage and confidence to face people.

"The schools also make you a part of the old-boy network, which will always help you out when in need. For example, jobs are always found for you. You don't have too much trouble, because people tend to know you fairly well. It's as if you're one of the family. It's very important to remember this, because one day they may well need your help, too.

"Essentially, it's the whole class structure. You hear of brother helping brother, man helping man, old schoolboy helping old schoolboy. Just like any gentlemen's club in London, membership goes not by who you are but by who you know. Very few nouveau riche would attain their position without a reasonable boarding-school education. It's terribly important, and it gives a sense of belonging. The British have always had this need to be part of a group or a team. There are individuals who stand out from the rest, usually because of the bounding confidence that a boarding-school education gives them. They enjoy a sense of belonging to old England, and, let's face it, we have plenty of history."

This sense of social position is often mirrored in the actual physical environment, and the best British schools—that is, the oldest British schools—are dominated by images of grand and ancient stone halls, properly dressed students debating important subjects in measured tones, and premonitions of leadership yet to emerge from within the classrooms. As Andrew relates it, "The whole place just reeks of centuries of education and the famous people who have passed through its halls—the old-boy networks that were born in schools like this. British boarding schools have immense history and beauty. They are invariably set in remarkable grounds which today, I'm afraid, money couldn't buy. They give you this sense of history. Also dominance. And power to believe in what you want to do without question, to get on with your life without letting other people interfere. Old ties still run very strong in this country. People will help you if you're an old schoolboy. It creates a great sense of security.

"It does one good to go away to boarding school. It teaches independence and great strength of character. Above all, it teaches you to be yourself and not be shy in the face of adversity. You must have courage in everything that you do and say. And if you believe that you are right, you must stick to your word. This, I'm afraid, is

Roy Massey, Choir Master of Hereford Cathedral, says of the regimen: "The boys work very hard. They do a full school program and eighteen hours a week as a member of the choir...some of the great orchestral players and conductors started life in this way."

OPPOSITE: *Choir boy at Winchester Cathedral*

something that can only be gained by a boarding-school education. I feel it's a great pity that not everybody can afford one."

While no one will dispute that the public-school system affords a first-class education to young scholars, the downside is the system's emotional toll. Englishman Ivor Cutler describes how deeply the rigidity of the British educational system pervades the sensibility of its countrymen: "In Britain, men, in the main, have been brought up to keep a stiff upper lip, never let their emotions show, and never show affection. This means that when two men meet, they are unable to throw their arms around one another and give one another a kiss. They're almost obliged to punch one another, hard, and to swear at one another. This passes for affection. It all started with the public-school system where poor little children were sent off at a very young age, away from their parents, and put into this frightening jungle—nursery school—and told that if you cry, you're a sissy."

Psychoanalyst Ean Begg confirms that the British educational system exacts a grave psychological toll on the English gentleman. "Something happened in the nineteenth century to kill or dampen the English spirit, and I think it was the public-school system with its idea of the gentleman and serving the Empire. That meant putting a brake on the emotions, and so one's sorrows had to be carried out privately. Generally, if you wanted to cry, you had to go to the lavatory to do it.

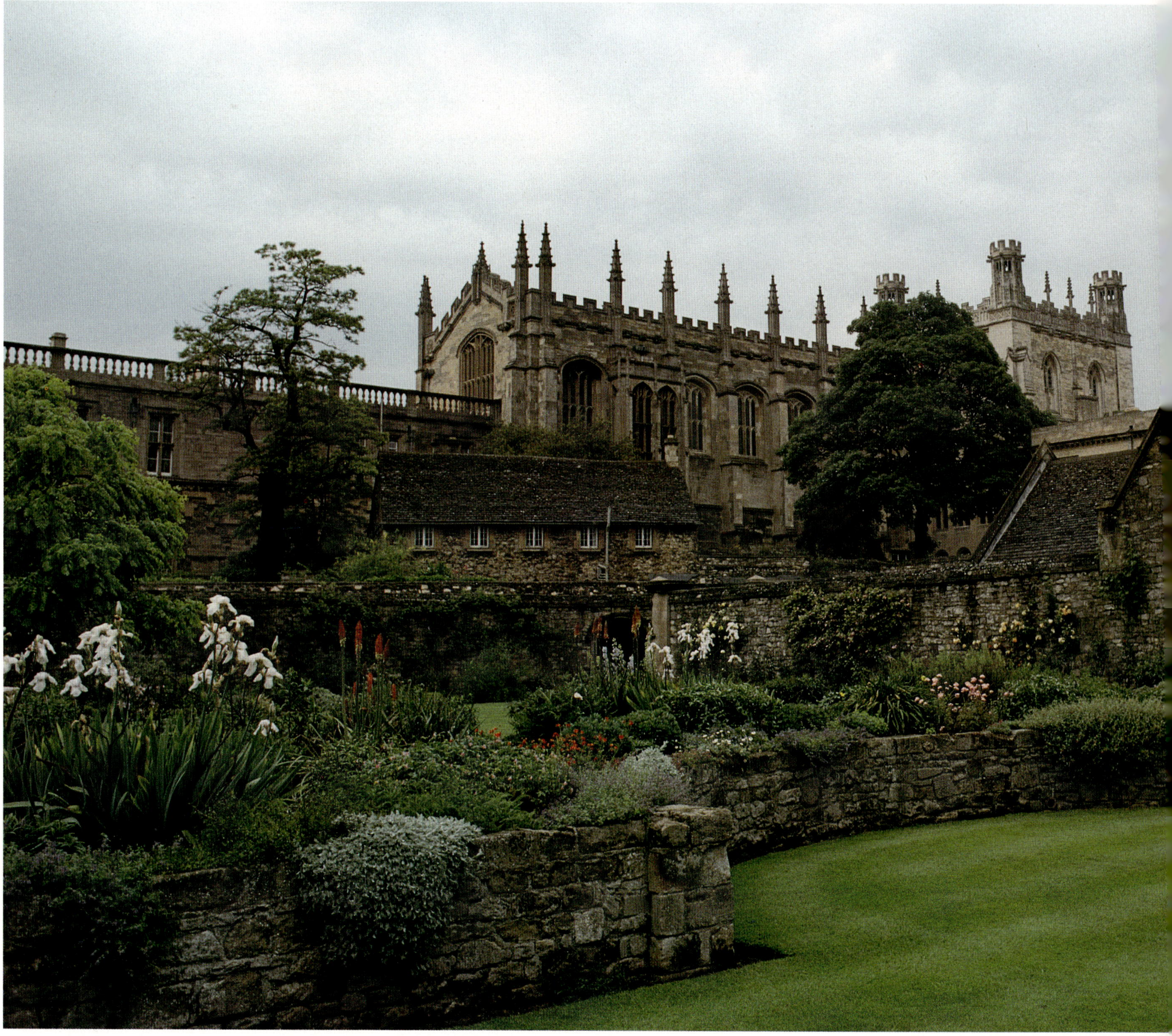

"Of course, men and women are very different beings, but it seems to me that in England they're even more strangers to one another than in other countries. This is because there's such a taboo on feeling. Typically, what happens is the man says, 'Yes, darling, everything is wonderful. Everything is fine. No, I've got no complaints at all.' Until one day, he finds his wife has walked out on him. She can't stand any longer this total lack of ability to talk about feelings."

Oxbridge

Oxford and Cambridge, often jointly referred to as Oxbridge, are the two oldest universities in the English-speaking world. Together, they have exerted a profound influence on the development of society and government in Great Britain, one that is perhaps unparalleled by any

ABOVE: *The door to the Deanery Garden where college tutor Charles Dodgson met and played with Alice Liddell, daughter of the Dean of Christ Church. The imaginative stories told by Dodgson and inspired by Alice led to his penning the immortal "Alice in Wonderland," under the name of Lewis Carroll.*

LEFT: *Christ Church, Oxford University*

other institution in the world. From their beginnings, in about 1167 and 1209 respectively, until 1821, they were the only universities in England. Their alumni include almost everyone of importance in British letters and politics—the most notable exception being William Shakespeare.

As a result of their roles in cultivating the elite in British society and an attendant attitude of self-importance, Oxford and Cambridge are viewed ambivalently by many Britons. This mixed attitude is subtly described by author Robertson Davies in *The Manticore:*

> Father had always assumed I would go to the University of Toronto, but I wanted to go to Oxford, and he jumped at that... [H]e had romantic ideas about universities, and Oxford appealed to him. So I went there, and because Father wanted me to be in a big college, I got into Christ Church.
>
> People are always writing in their memoirs about what Oxford meant to them. I can't pretend the place itself meant extraordinary things to me. Of course it was pleasant, and I liked the interesting buildings; architectural critics are always knocking

Christ Church, Oxford, established by Henry VIII in 1546 as both college and cathedral. It has been said: "There is absolutely no separation between them as if they were two distinct members in one and the same body."

RIGHT: *Oxford University*

OPPOSITE: *A college gate at Oxford University*

them, but after Toronto they made my eyes pop. They spoke of an idea of education strange to me; discomfort there was, but no meanness, no hint of edification on the cheap. And I like the feel of a city of youth, which is what Oxford seems to be, though anybody with eyes in his head can see that it is run by old men. But my Oxford was a post-war Oxford, crammed to the walls and rapidly growing into a big industrial city. And there was much criticism of the privilege it implied, mostly from people who were sitting bang in the middle of the privilege and getting all they could out of it.

Catering to the needs of the privileged few has been the ideological foundation of Oxford and Cambridge as well as the focus of much controversy. From the beginning, entrance into these institutions was a privilege reserved for the upper classes. Government reforms, designed to favor individuals of merit rather than status, only contributed to the fixity of the establishment as students from Oxbridge passed easily into the highest ranks of the British civil service and thereby dominated government. Between 1870 and 1913, fifty-seven of the sixty-one men appointed to the Treasury were university graduates, and all but three came from either Oxford or Cambridge.

It is no wonder, then, that the schools are the focus and the whipping post of what one British historian has described as "the appalling British obsession with class."

Winchester

While it is true that children of privilege are in the best position to attain an education, it is also true that there are simply not enough openings available for everyone—rich and poor—who desires to go to school. One Winchester student claims, "In this country, fourteen percent of the people are educated in the university, whereas in places like Germany, it's much higher. I mean, in Germany there are so many people either trying to get into universities or already there that they have to throw dice to see who can get the accommodations, but in this country there is no real opportunity."

Ramifications of this statistic are evident to everyone within Britain's educational system. Former Westminster headmaster John Rae explains how the system inhibits any ambition the less privileged student might harbor for a better education:

"About a month ago, I went into a comprehensive school on an estate in South London. I was doing a project there, and I found that the young men and women had no hopes at all. They were born poor, born into the wrong class. They are not stupid—they know the

Chapel at Cambridge University

OPPOSITE: *The Great Hall, Christ Church, Oxford, where the Dean, Canons, Students and undergraduates of the House dine during the Full Term*

score—but there is no hope for them. I went to the school's headmaster, a black headmaster, who came over to this country with the first wave of immigrants, and he told me that the children sometimes have unrealistic expectations. 'Our job,' and I quote him, 'is to lower their horizons.' And that seems to be a motto for what's going on in Britain."

Another student confirms Rae's observations: "You ask people what their ambitions are, and they say, 'Well, we'll go out with our friends and, you know, have a nice Saturday night.' The jobs they can expect to get aren't really worth writing home about. And there's a general feeling that we're not going to get any higher. I mean, you drive through the town square, and you see groups of children our age just standing about, sort of in the rain. They don't have anywhere else to go."

According to Rae, the reason for this sense of hopelessness stems, in part, from the ever-present problem of the class system: "The class system, which we pretend is a thing of the past, is still there. And Winchester, the original public school in English history, the great school, is nevertheless now helping to perpetuate this class system."

Music rehearsal at Winchester College

RIGHT: *Three Winchester students participating in a debate on the issue of public versus private education in Great Britain*

Ironically, Winchester College was originally established, as Second Master Stephen Winkley recalls, to "educate poor boys in such a way that they would grow up to take a part in the life of the church, which was where clever people were needed at that time. We were set up [in 1393] in the aftermath of the Black Death by prelate William of Wykeham, who was himself a poor boy.

"A lot of the boys we educate pay large sums of money in fees, so I suppose technically speaking we're not doing quite as well as he would have liked. This worries me, because I'm sure there are lots of poor children out there who would do very well if they came here. Clever boys, who are probably rather bored and frustrated at their lack of progress and not being taken seriously, may feel that their cleverness is being taken for granted. If they came here, they would get stretched and pushed and encouraged in a way that other schools possibly couldn't do. Also—and this is very important for a clever child—they would be with other clever children.

"Most of the boys who come to Winchester expect that education will do something for them. That may be something rather low-level, such as get them good A levels [the advanced General Certificate of Education exam] in the university place. For lots of them, it will mean more than that—it will mean opening lots of doors. That's a view of education that isn't very widely shared by educators and by victims of education in the rest of the country."

Winkley's views on education in Great Britain are closely related to his views on society in general: "I came into teaching at the end of the sixties, and as everybody says these days, it was an exciting time to be in education, because the children one taught really thought that the world could be changed and that there were no limits to the number of things you could do with your life. Then suddenly—and I don't think this has anything to do with a particular sort of Tory government; I think it's much more to do with economic realities, that is, the oil-price change and things of that kind—suddenly, the children I taught began to get awfully nervous. One began to find—and I still find this—that they dream of safety. Now that seems to me a rather sad notion, that idealistic and potentially idealistic young people with an enormous amount to contribute look forward to a life when they'll be safe. They'll have a safe house and a safe wife and children and a jolly nice job, and all will be well. It's a bit alarming and it's a bit disappointing."

In the end, William of Wykeham's dream of educating poor but clever boys to be leaders of their country may not be realized within the confines of the current educational system. One Winchester student suggests the futility of such an ambition: "The question is whether we can use our education here and the skills that we have picked up to change that in some way. At the moment, it strikes me that people who are well educated just become part of the system. They just go off and get good jobs in the city or the civil service or whatever, but it takes the single revolutionary to actually set things going."

Winkley expresses a somewhat ambivalent view of the overall system: "I think that what we stand for at Winchester College is a long tradition of individual development, of boys being able to find their way through a mass of opportunities to discover something about themselves that is good and that can be better. The people who get through the system, who struggle their way up from difficult circumstances such as impoverishment and deprivation, the people who do get through, tend to be marvelous.

"I feel sad, though, because there are enormous intellectual talents in this country that are not being used as well as they might. As a result, clever people often feel rather disenchanted and uncommitted to making this country work."

Student in military exercise at Winchester College, the oldest public school in England still inhabited. Public schools are the equivalent of private schools in America.

A working-class neighborhood in Birmingham, England

Birmingham

Barrister Nigel Fraser is one of the few people to have overcome the odds and made it. The son of Afro-Caribbean immigrants, Fraser was born in the tough and gritty environment of Birmingham, Great Britain's second largest city.

Fraser attended the Ladywood Comprehensive School—the equivalent of an American public high school—and overcame pointed suggestions to "lower his horizons." Addressing students at his alma mater, he recalled his earliest yearnings to break the mould:

"I remember I was in the careers room. There was a careers lecturer, and everyone was putting up their hands and saying, 'What do you have to do to become a motor mechanic? or What do you have to do to get the usual working-class jobs?'

"I'm not saying there's anything wrong with that, because someone has to do those jobs, and they're important. But I put up my hand and said, 'Sir, what do you have to do to become a barrister?' All my mates and everyone around me started to laugh like it was a big joke, and I felt discouraged. But I knew it came from the way we were conditioned to think. We were *taught* to think in those terms.

"When I was in the fifth form, I had three choices: work in a factory, remain unemployed, or turn to crime. A fourth choice, joining a profession, wasn't a possibility by virtue of my surroundings. I didn't want to work in a factory; I didn't want to be unemployed; I didn't want to go to prison, like a lot of people in my community. I wanted to be somebody. I wanted to contribute something to society, to help people. I decided to become a barrister because I thought: 'Why can't I do that? I'm as much entitled as anyone else.' "

One of Fraser's former teachers explains why educators are reluctant to encourage even those with promise: "I feel strongly against giving people targets they'll never

Students at the Ladywood Comprehensive School in Birmingham. Comprehensive schools are the equivalent of public schools in America.

be able to meet, encouraging people when I know all it's going to mean is terrible disappointment. Because not only do you have your failures but you lose a trust that you had before. They think, 'Well, that woman told me that, or that man told me that. I trusted him or her, and they've let me down.' That's the thing I worry about. A lot of people don't make it." Students accept this rationale with little resistance, for virtually nothing in their experience appears to contradict it.

Fraser's most significant barrier—class—was, in his case, compounded by a lack of resources. "The first time I met barristers was when I joined the profession. All those kinds of people were remote to me growing up in a working-class setting in Hansworth. If you're born into a certain social class, you're going to be limited; you're

Barrister Nigel Fraser, a graduate of the Ladywood School

compelled to actually remain in that circle and learn its values.

"I come from a large family. I went to a local primary school. In the area where I grew up, there were a lot of problems. People used to get into trouble with the police. I wanted to be somebody. I wanted to be respected for what I was and for doing the job I chose. But most of all, I wanted to live a comfortable life, an affluent life. I don't mind saying so. I don't think there's anything wrong in being comfortable or well off, as long as it doesn't get to you or you don't tread on other people's toes.

"When I was fourteen or fifteen, I wanted to live in a really nice house, drive a nice car, and have a substantial income and a good amount of money in the bank. Those things are important to me. My mother and father came to this country with two suitcases in their hands. They had nothing. They had to start from scratch and struggle to bring up a large family.

"We didn't go hungry. We weren't short of anything, but it was always the basics. And what you don't have you don't miss, so within that situation I was happy. But now I would like to be comfortable. I don't want to live a poor life.

"It was a big task for a working-class person from Ladywood to become a barrister. I managed through sheer strength, determination, resilience, and belief in my ability. But it was a struggle! I tell you it was war! It was like living in a concrete jungle! Don't let anyone fool you. It was like hell. All I can advise is: have dreams and work hard to aim for those dreams."

Fraser's bold steps into the mainstream of British history anticipate a renewal of Britain along more egalitarian lines. He encourages the students from Ladywood by telling them, "I really do hope in another ten years time, if the school is still here—and I sincerely hope it will be—that quite a number of you young people will be sitting where I am and speaking to future barristers and doctors or whatever you want to be."

Nigel Fraser in "Chambers," London

London

When a man is tired of London, he is tired of life, for there is in London all that life can afford.

—SAMUEL JOHNSON (1709–1784)

London, at the height of the British Empire in the nineteenth century, was perhaps the closest thing to a world capital that civilization has ever known. Founded as a commercial city after the Roman conquest in the first century, its situation on the River Thames, roughly fifty miles from the sea, quickly made it an important port for trade between Britain and the rest of the Roman Empire. Aided by an elaborate system of roads, which the Romans directed toward London, the city also became the center of commerce within Britain itself.

London commerce was, in fact, directly responsible for the development of the British Empire. England's imperial ambitions were spurred by London merchants in search of new markets and raw materials. It is largely due to London-based monopolies in the sixteenth century—the Muscovy Company, the Levant Company, and the East India Company—that British expansion proved so formidable. The case of the East India Company is instructive, for it was their agents who established British administration in India. It was not until the mid-nineteenth century that an office of Indian affairs was established in the Foreign Office. As one veteran of the Empire in India put it, "The English never sought an empire. They never set out to create one. They didn't want it. But when they woke up one day and found an empire had somehow come, they did their best to rule it well."

While no longer the center of a great empire, London remains the most important transportation hub within the country. Evocatively named train stations such as Victoria, Waterloo, and Paddington serve as departure points for all corners of Great Britain and facilitate con-

Big Ben

OPPOSITE: *Statue of Winston Churchill, Parliament Square*

nections to ferries bound for the ports of continental Europe. Once the construction of a tunnel under the English Channel is completed, the historic link between Great Britain and the rest of the world will have its most modern example.

As a city, London is replete with symbols of the greatness of the Empire. Lucinda Sieger, a Glasgow-born singer who has lived in London for ten years, admits that "the symbols of Britain always come back to London—Big Ben, Parliament, the Queen. They are what people see as the symbols of London. But," she adds, "there's a lot more to it. There's a lot of cultures, a lot of races, and a lot going on in London."

If England is often called "a nation of shopkeepers," then London is surely the shop: display window, front office, and cash register all in one. Although the products

Although some might demur, Royalty has its pragmatic uses for the English. The extravagance associated with the Royal Family—e.g., the Changing of the Guard at Buckingham Palace, the Queen's residence in London, the Crown Jewels in the Tower of London, and the occasional Royal wedding—attract an extraordinary number of tourists eager to witness traditions of great endurance and antiquity. For the British themselves, especially the English, Royalty symbolizes the Empire's former magnificence and the continued vitality of the nation.

As one Englishwoman puts it, "It's simply pride. I think people enjoy the pomp and ceremony of the monarch. It's like the Romans: if the people are really miserable, give them another circus; you know, let them see something. We enjoy seeing our Queen walk around in a

Attending services at Westminster Cathedral on Commonwealth Day (May 24), the anniversary of Queen Victoria's birth

may differ from the days of Samuel Johnson, the terms of sale are still the same, and no matter where you are in England, you have to come to London if you want to make it. Lucinda observes, "London is a marketplace for everyone's wares—designers, craftsmen, whatever you are. I am a commodity and I come down here to sell what I do. This is where the record companies are, the galleries for artists. It's the best place in Britain."

Pomp and Ceremony

"There is something about Royalty that's hard to define," says Ivor Spencer. "I would say they're as near to God as you can possibly get. We know that they're not God, but somehow they're right up there. The aristocracy is another level, but I think this country would suffer terribly if we didn't have Royalty."

OPPOSITE: *Royal Horse Guard, Clarence House, the London residence of the Queen Mother*

Changing of the Guard, Buckingham Palace, the London Palace of Her Majesty Queen Elizabeth II

dress with five million diamonds sewn on it. Most of us realize that we are never going to have that much cash or wear all those lovely frocks and jewelry. But we can appreciate it, you see.

"We only start to resent things when they are just slightly beyond our range. I don't like people with Volvos and stuff, but I don't mind the Queen living in Buckingham Palace. I think we like the Royal Family because they say something about us. You see, we're very proud as a nation. The monarchy sort of represents or crystallizes those feelings far more than a parliament could ever do."

Seemingly extravagant sums of monies are spent on the monarch and on fairy-tale-style events, yet no one seems to mind. Most feel that the importance lies in the continuation of tradition. As one admirer of the Queen explained, "I like the pomp and ceremony. I get pretty emotional when I see the Queen on the television. I don't know why. Back in my psyche somewhere it makes me want to cry when I see the Queen. I like the thought of having a monarchy. I think you'll find that the majority of people do, too.

"Someone once said, 'By the year 2000 there will be five kings: hearts, spades, clubs, diamonds, and England.' I like that. I like the thought of it as something as everlasting as a pack of cards. And I like the feeling of history and of things continuing on. A lot of people get a good feeling from thinking it won't change."

The head office of Lloyd's of London, the world's largest insurance market

Big Ben and the Houses of Parliament

London's Theater district

Theater

"The English are very reserved, even when they go to the theater. I remember seeing a Spanish company come over with this fantastic show, and at the end of this incredible performance, the audience waited for somebody to start clapping. It's what an English audience is all about. They're very inhibited and can't show their appreciation immediately, and I think that's in everything."

LUCINDA SIEGER, *London artist*

The Globe Theater, Soho

Piccadilly Circus

The Tower Bridge, London

Black cabs neatly lined up in front of a taxi restaurant in London

Signs

The sights and sounds of London are unique, capturing a flavor and flair that are distinctly English. Psychoanalyst Ean Begg explains one of the more obvious English idiosyncrasies: "One characteristic that never fails to strike the foreigner is the orderly queuing that goes on—not always at football matches but at bus stops and in shops. This, really, is knowing your place. No pushing forward. And it's a very useful way of being in an overcrowded world. However, it denies individual self-expression, and the English, no less than anybody else, need and wish for this.

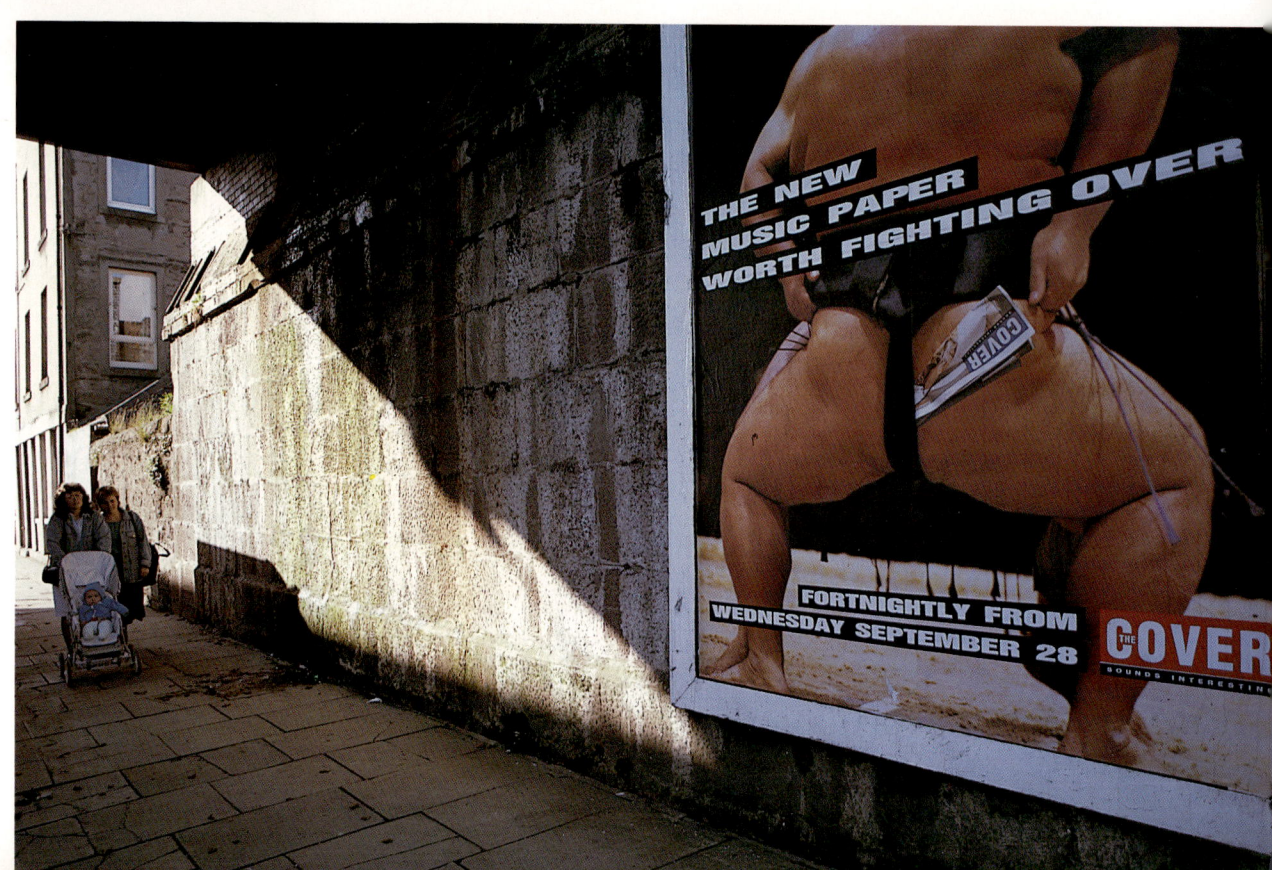

"The English go to extremes to prevent self-revelation and to prevent conflict. For example, in officers' messes in the army, at prewar dinner parties, and at colleges at Oxford and Cambridge, you were not allowed to talk about women, politics, or religion. That is, you couldn't talk about sex and money, and if you talked about religion, you were dubbed a religious maniac. Don't be enlightened, and don't talk about anything important. Tell stories and talk about the weather or sports or books if they're not too controversial. So an almost Japanese-like rigidity of nonrevelation and nonfriction is part of the English character."

> *But now behold,*
> *In the quick forge and working-horse of thought,*
> *How London does pour out her citizens.*
>
> —WILLIAM SHAKESPEARE (1564–1616), HENRY IV

To outsiders—even those such as Glasgow-born Lucinda Sieger who have made London their home for a long time—the English can be a very withdrawn, intense people. "Everyone is sort of into getting on with their own lives. They're quite withdrawn and hard to approach. There are a lot of cultures here, but the English are a very hard race to know. You can live down here for some time and work with people, but you don't actually know them. They don't give that much away.

The London marketplace

87

With London traffic among the world's worst, motorcycle messengers have become a familiar and often dangerous sight on the streets of London. Dressed in imposing black leather, motorcycle boots and helmuts, these "road warriors" have been sighted at speeds up to 120 mph.

"Looking around London from wherever I may be, I see people who are very reserved and inhibited. The clubs are full of young, hungry people looking for something new. They are dancing out there late at night. London is a city which attracts people from all around the world, and I see London opening up and looking to the outside world for inspiration."

Psychoanalyst Ean Begg offers an explanation for the infamous British reserve: "To begin with, there is a conditioning that feelings are not to be expressed after a certain age. It was once said to me that the kindest thing an English mother can say about her child is 'You wouldn't know he was there.' Children here are to be seen and not heard, not in restaurants, not in public. They are hived off with nannies in nurseries and sent off to boarding schools at the age of eight and bigger public schools at the age of thirteen. This conditioning produces an overadapted person, a conformist who knows his place in the class system and who doesn't rock the boat, who knows what the game is and plays it."

Begg cites this example: "An intense love and need for

privacy is one of the factors that has come out of living on an overcrowded island, and it spills over into the life of the home. An Englishman's home is his castle. The father has his own place where he sits and reads the papers, and it's 'Don't bother your father, he's busy now.' And his relationship with his wife will have to be carried out in code—that is, there are certain things you can talk about and certain things you can't.

"The feeling world is left behind at the age of four or five. You know, many grown Englishmen still get a tremendous release from playing with toy trains or teddy bears."

In Hyde Park, Londoners often come to sit, stroll or perhaps listen to the "tub-thumping" public orators who gather near Marble Arch and air their views while standing on soap boxes. Along with the raucous House of Commons, Marble Arch is one of the last places where the English tradition of passionate vocal protest is still honored.

Hyde Park

*And dream of London, small and white and clean,
The clear Thames bordered by its gardens green.*

—WILLIAM MORRIS (1834–1896), THE WANDERERS

The British love of nature is no less evident in London's Hyde Park than in the rolling downs of Dorset. Londoner Andrew Thompson speaks about his particular affinity: "I often come here to Hyde Park, in the center of London, to just lie and relax and generally piece myself together and wind down after a busy day. It's a beautiful place with many different sorts of people walking about it. I always find it best to bring along a little music and plug in to cut out the drone of the traffic, which is only a few yards away.

"I usually listen to Mozart, who in my opinion is one of the finest composers who ever lived. His music is light and enchanting. Being an oboist myself, I quite appreciate his style. Listening to classical music is a great family tradition for me. I attend a fair amount of concerts in London where there are many varied offerings, so you really can't go wrong.

"I notice the people who walk around the park—their insecurities and their values. In a place like this, you'll see all sorts of egos and temperaments, ranging from calm to apathetic. It's a pity but that's the way people have become. I think it's due to our increasingly hostile society where people feel constantly threatened and feel they have to defend themselves. It's a shame but that's the way it is."

A religious fanatic in London's Piccadilly Circus

OPPOSITE: *Demonstrators gather in Hyde Park in support of the Chinese students who occupied Beijing's Tienanmen Square for close to two months before being brutally dispersed by soldiers on June 4, 1989.*

"G Fawkes is innocent"—Guy Fawkes Day (November 5). In 1605, Guy Fawkes was arrested for his part in the Gunpowder Plot, an unsuccessful attempt to kill King James I and the Lords and Commons by blowing up Parliament.

RIGHT: *A bonfire in London's East End celebrating Guy Fawkes Day*

Collecting pennies on Guy Fawkes Day to buy firecrackers, a boy calls out:
"A penny for the guy."

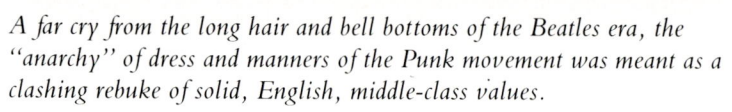

A far cry from the long hair and bell bottoms of the Beatles era, the "anarchy" of dress and manners of the Punk movement was meant as a clashing rebuke of solid, English, middle-class values.

OVERLEAF LEFT: *Michelle Caines, legal secretary by day, "goth" by night (the word "goth" comes from gothic and is used to suggest the tone and character of being a Punk)*

OVERLEAF RIGHT: *A London policeman, known as "bobby"*

97

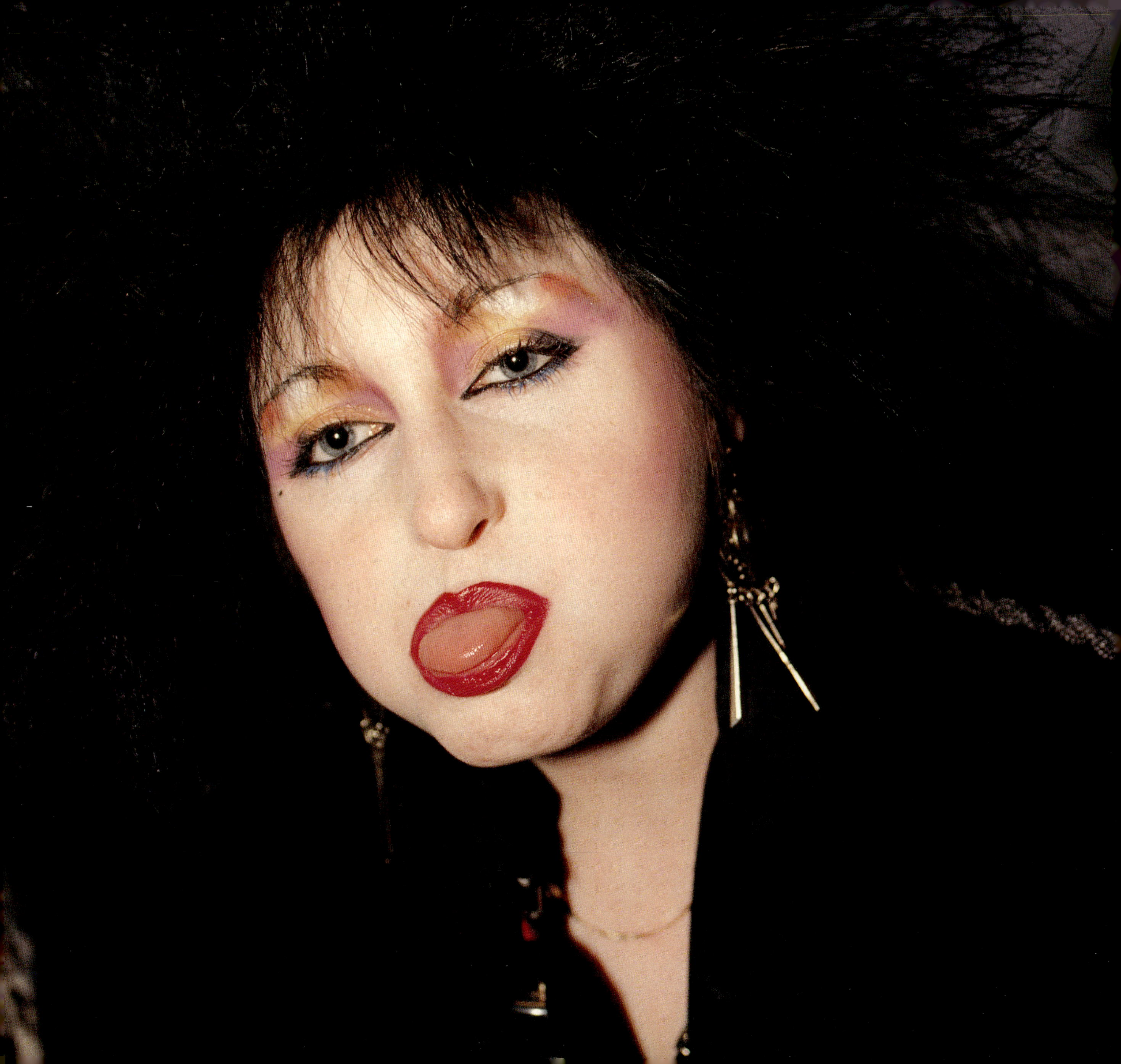

99

Commonwealth

In the years since World War II, the British Empire has all but disbanded. As a young English boy scout puts it, "There isn't much of us left, is there? There are a few red dots in the middle of the Pacific, and that's about it. But we don't need to think about the Empire. We need to think about the world—the global village."

'Global village' is an apt description. As the British Empire contracted, it was slowly transformed into a commonwealth of nations composed of countries—forty-nine at last count—that were formerly dominions, colonies, or territories and that now frequently come together to discuss issues of mutual concern—their sole common denominator being the fact that, whether in Asia, the Americas, or Africa, they were all once the subjects of the Queen.

The rise of the Commonwealth has wrought a remarkable change on the face of Britain itself. Where once the trilby hat and tightly furled umbrella were the only familiar badges of an Englishman, today these symbols are joined by the kaffiyeh and the turban. In past centuries, young Britons sailed away in search of new opportunities. Ironically, former citizens of the Empire now flock back to the British Isles to seek their fortune. All the while, Britain struggles to maintain its identity as it copes with forces that threaten to make it as much a melting pot of the world's people as the United States.

Faces of the Commonwealth

A clear example of Britain's attempt to cope with its ethnic diversity is television's Channel 4, which was established to cater to the interests of its myriad minorities. As explained by Farouk Dhondi, whose own family was split between royalists in favor of British rule in India and nationalists in the mold of Mahatma Ghandi: "Part of the effort of Channel 4 was to appoint a particular person to look after the interests, subjects, culture, and so on, of the ethnic minorities in Britain, which means Indians, Pakistanis, Bangladeshis, Sri Lankans, Africans, Cypriots, Chinese, and West Indians of all sorts—Jamaicans, Trinidadians, Guyanese, Barandians. You can make a larger list, but those are the main categories. And there is programming of all sorts—drama series, chat shows, and current-affairs magazines aimed at particular audiences."

It is interesting to note the experiences of immigrants who were more directly influenced by the British colonials than they were by their own people—even while still in their native lands. One particular West Indian, a resident of Britain for more than thirty years and an immigration officer, explains: "I grew up in a family that knew very little other than an English form of culture.

Major Narinda Saroop

RIGHT: *The Rt. Hon. Cecil Parkinson addressing members of The Durbar Club, founded by Major Saroop in 1981*

We ate most of the same things that one eats in England. My background was very Scottish. The matter of color never entered into our minds or heads.

"The Empire as it was then was a wonderful thing. As a boy I remember going frequently to the beach and looking north and thinking that one day I would come to Britain and see the mother country, as it was then known. Of course, in schools we were taught more about the geography of Britain than about our own countries. One sang songs about Britain and learnt about the economy, the food, and the leisure-time activities of English people. One acquired a feeling of Englishness that is very difficult to explain. And one longed to see this in reality.

"In spite of the institution which some now believe to be responsible for our culture's lack of development, it would be true to say that the Empire created feelings of love and affection, not only for Britain but for other members of the Commonwealth. When West Indians began coming to Britain in fairly large numbers, it would be true to say that they loved the English to an extent that was difficult for the English to quite appreciate. However, I think there are complementary bits of character, temperament, and inclinations between the British and Indians."

One man whose life straddles Indian and British culture is Major Narinda Saroop, soldier, businessman, and heir to the aristocratic traditions of both countries. He has used his position specifically to promote greater participation of minorities in Britain. In 1981, he founded the Durbar Club "to provide a forum for the more thinking leaders of the Asian community in this country to exchange views, get their points across to the leading members of the Tory party, and meet their counterparts in the social and business life of Great Britain."

While he is active in the political life of Great Britain and would like to see greater involvement on the part of other minorities, Major Saroop acknowledges that there

Ivor Spencer instructing trainees in the art and philosophy of being the perfect English butler

have been some formidable obstacles to overcome. "Until the late seventies, I would have said that the majority of the Asian community was, quite rightly, mostly involved with earning money and getting security, and therefore it probably wasn't right to expect them to take part in politics. I can imagine and understand the reluctance of somebody who doesn't look local to knock on doors and canvass and do all the humdrum activities that are part of political life. But I'm sure that will change."

Indeed, change is inevitable not only for members of the Indian community but for all Commonwealth citizens of Britain. As a colleague of Major Saroop has noted, "It's often forgotten that the strength and progress of this country has been founded upon immigration and integration since the earliest waves—wave after wave of new people coming in and being assimilated into what seemed an established culture."

Beaulieu

*The Stately Homes of England
How beautiful they stand,
To prove the upper classes
Have still the upper hand.*

—NOEL COWARD (1899–1973),
THE STATELY HOMES OF ENGLAND

The archway of the Beaulieu Abbey, originally a Cistercian monastery founded by King John in 1204

RIGHT: *Presently the residence of Lord Montagu, Third Baron of Beaulieu, the large gatehouse was originally converted into a dwelling house in 1538.*

OPPOSITE: *Nightfall at Beaulieu*

*From *The Stately Homes of England* by Noel Coward
© 1950 Chappell Music Ltd. All rights reserved. Used by permission.

One of the enduring curiosities of late-twentieth-century Britain is the survival of the landed aristocracy, complete with inherited titles. For many, land and title represent a tangible link to Britain's glorious past. Unfortunately, members of the landed aristocracy presently face serious financial hardships as a result of inheritance taxes levied on estates as they pass from one generation to the next. Yet the idea of either selling or allowing family land to pass to the state, where it would be subject to untold divisions and mutilations, remains unbearable—not only to the titleholders but to many working-class people as well.

Even before the imposition of taxes, many family estates were opened for public viewing in an effort to raise money for upkeep—a practice that was both popular and productive. In the nineteenth century, for example, Chatsworth House, seat of the Duke of Devonshire, attracted eighty thousand visitors a year. Since World War II, more and more houses have been opened to visitors. Today, there are roughly one hundred private houses accessible to the public. While many might find the prospect of "living above the shop" unsettling, such considerations are overridden by a profound attachment to the land, especially when one's home really is a castle.

The instinct to preserve these bonds to the land is articulated by Edward John Barrington Douglas-Scott-Montagu, third and present Baron Montagu of Beaulieu (pronounced BYOO-lee). His impeccable lineage includes two lords, five dukes, two earls, and four kings. His ancestral estate at Beaulieu includes the National Motor

Museum and is one of the country's most popular attractions.

"I think unless your own family have lived in a place for generations," says Lord Montagu, "it's very difficult to understand the deep emotional attachment we feel to our homes. We feel we belong to our possessions rather than our possessions belong to us."

Every year half a million people visit Beaulieu. "We are the most commercial private house in the country," claims Lady Montagu. "I don't think I know of any other house that's open to the public all year round. We're open seven days a week...psychologically, it's absolutely relentless." Despite being on permanent view, Lord Montagu would do anything before he would abandon

Peter Murfin, Beaulieu gamekeeper

OPPOSITE TOP: *The National Motor Museum, which includes a monorail, is located on the Beaulieu grounds and is one of the country's most popular tourist attractions.*

OPPOSITE BOTTOM: *Lady Montagu of Beaulieu*

Beaulieu. "I think the past is very much present. You can't really look at one's family history over five hundred years and just throw it away. I despise those people who have done so. I think it is well worth the fight. And, of course, it is a very beautiful place."

The Baron's respect for the sanctity of the land is shared by Peter Murfin, one of the four gamekeepers who oversee the approximately thirteen thousand acres comprising the Beaulieu estate. Murfin's job, as he describes it, is "to keep the balance. Although my name is gamekeeper, I'm more of a naturalist."

For Murfin, protecting the land from poachers and predators is not just a job. "It's a way of life. And that is the only way you can describe it. You're on duty twenty-four hours a day, seven days a week—eight if there was eight. It's marvelous really."

Though the pay is low and the hours long, Murfin harbors no ill feelings toward the owners of Beaulieu. "I look at the aristocrats as people who have had money and handed it down to their sons or daughters. They've managed to keep it going. People who have recently made a lot of money really look down on the general public, which in my opinion is all wrong. Proper aristocrats, used to having money, are proper ladies and gentlemen."

Lord Montagu would hardly dispute this view of the upper classes. "May I remind you," he says, "of what aristocracy actually means? Discreet word, it means *rule of the best*."

The concept of a ruling class does not present any problem for Peter Murfin. "On the Beaulieu estate, I get on very, very well with all of them," he claims. "I know I'm working-class. I don't try to put on airs and graces. There's a place for everybody. I treat everybody as normal, whether they're gentry, royalty, or whatever. When we meet, it always tip me hat, 'Good morning, Sir... Me Lord... Your Grace,' or whatever, and then we just chat away. The way I look at it, if you can keep your place you can't look down on yourself. As long as we understand the way things are and behave ourselves and treat everyone as they are, then we get on."

Murfin supports the tradition of inherited land, mainly because it protects his beloved countryside from overdevelopment. "I think England is too highly populated for the area that we've got. If it wasn't for the aristocrats keeping or trying to keep the estates together, then you'd get people saying, 'Oh, I like that area, I'll buy a little bit and have a house built there.' This is how it goes. I've just come down from London, and all you have there is a concrete jungle."

The Valley Gardens

*Our England is a garden that is full of stately views,
Of borders, beds and shrubberies and lawns and avenues,
With statues on the terraces and peacocks strutting by;
But the Glory of the Garden lies in more than meets the eye.*

—RUDYARD KIPLING (1865–1936), THE GLORY OF THE GARDEN

Formal gardens were introduced to England by the Romans, who had long cultivated a taste for such refinements in their native land. But it wasn't until the eighteenth century that respected landscape gardeners such as "Capability" Brown transformed landscaping into a distinctive English art form. The continental taste, dictated primarily by the French, favored carefully constructed geometrical patterns of flowers, hedges, and trees. The *jardin anglais,* as it came to be known, glorified a more organic aesthetic, and whole estates were remodeled, hills flattened or raised, and streams, lakes, and cascades created.

Although the most spectacular English gardens are usually found on private estates, they are not simply follies of the rich. As one Londoner observes, "Having a garden is just part of English life." Whether tended in small villages and towns, behind simple row houses in the inner cities, or on the grounds of modest cottages in the countryside, gardens offer a respite from the hustle and bustle of everyday life and cast a serene spell over the land.

"My garden is always a pleasure," says Rachel Marchant, who cultivates her garden in Folkestone, a small town southeast of London. "It's a wonderful relaxation. Time spent in the garden is a chance to forget all your worries and troubles. It's such a source of enjoyment and beauty. Everyone gardens."

One of the most spectacular gardens in England is at Windsor Great Park, which surrounds the Queen's of-

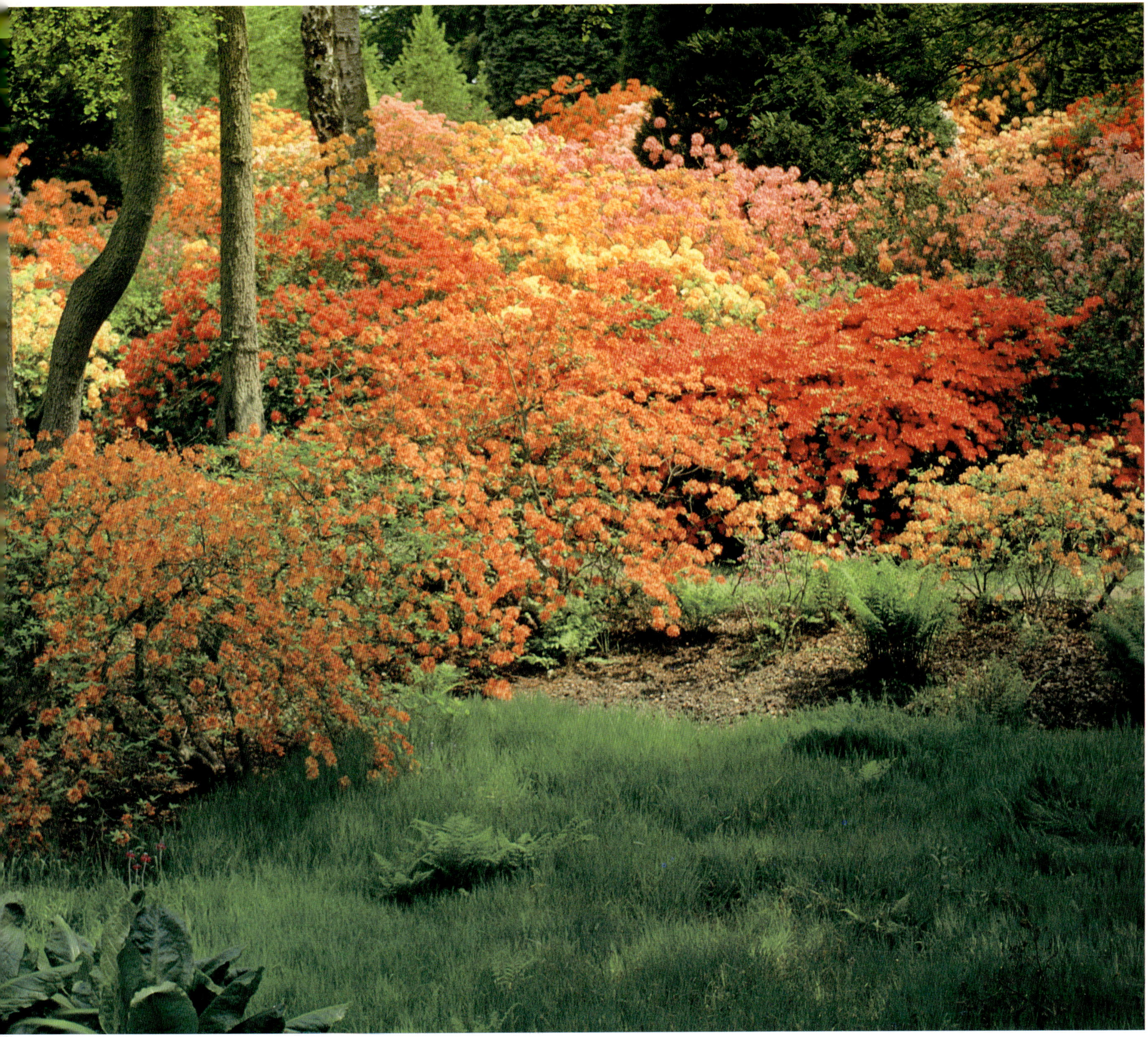

ficial residence at Windsor Castle. The castle is perhaps the finest royal residence in the world. It is the largest still inhabited and is surrounded by two thousand acres of rolling countryside. Windsor Great Park is actually a remnant of the Royal Forest, described once as "the sanctuary and special delight of kings, where laying aside their cares, they withdraw to refresh themselves with a little hunting; there, away from the turmoils inherent in a court, they breathe the pleasure of natural freedom." The Royal Forests, which in the thirteenth century covered nearly a third of England, was subject to a rigid code of laws under the House of Normandy that guaranteed to preserve them as "the safe mansion of wild beasts."

Within Windsor Great Park are The Savill Garden and The Valley Gardens, which collectively boast the largest collection of rhododendrons in the world. The lush greenery and multitude of exotic flowers make these gardens one of the most popular tourist attractions in England.

Perhaps it is their love of gardens that makes the British so fascinated by the weather. As one British meteorologist explains: The British are always talking about the weather. We don't have climate in this country—we have weather, and it's constantly changing. The British are always armed with umbrellas. Virtually every day is different. We often have many days where one day is totally different from the next. For instance, only the other day, I was sunbathing; a few days before that, I was actually making a snowman in the garden.

"A great deal of weather lore has been built up. In fact, there are probably more expressions to do with the weather than any other subject. One that schoolchildren learn is 'Red sky at night, shepherd's delight. Red sky at morning, shepherd's warning.' There's a good deal of truth in that. Another is 'If a pond can bear the weight of the duck, after Christmas will be just sludge and muck,' meaning that cold weather before Christmas often is an indication of damp, mild weather after Christmas. One of my favorites is 'Mackerel sky, mackerel sky, never long wet, never long dry.' A mackerel sky is one of the most colorful skies of all because it looks like the scales of a fish.

"Of course, the British are always resolving to make the best of it. Even if there is a heavy rainstorm while they are at the seaside or enjoying a picnic, they're going to make the best of it. This is characteristic of the British people."

PAGES 108-111: *The Valley Gardens in Windsor Great Park, which surrounds Windsor Castle, the official residence of the Queen of England. Windsor is located on the Thames in Berkshire, central England.*

Cotswolds and Yorkshire

*And did those feet in ancient time
Walk upon England's mountains green?
And was the holy Lamb of God
On England's pleasant pastures seen?*

*And did the Countenance Divine
Shine forth upon our clouded hills?*

—WILLIAM BLAKE (1757–1827), MILTON

Great Britain's history is revealed in its great cities and monuments, its towering cathedrals and silent battlefields—all places bearing the distinct hand of man. Then there is the beauty of the rolling countryside, a great, changing sea of natural wonders. But it is the prosperity provided by the land in its many forms that has attracted farmers for centuries.

The land makes no distinction between nobleman and commoner, educated or poor. These days, one farmer might live in the roughest dwelling and possess only a single tractor, while another will be a university graduate administering his land with an efficiency founded on strict management principles.

John Cook, a Yorkshire farmer, explains: "Farmers in Britain completely cross the British class structure. If a chap says 'farmer,' you cannot say what part of the social sphere he would consider himself in. There are some farmers who are right at the very top—social grade A, very educated, big farms, probably very good businessmen with a lot of culture. And you get some who are totally inward-looking and are, unfortunately, right down at the bottom of the pile."

The average English farm is not very large, especially when compared to the enormous tracts of farmland found in North America. But the English are extremely productive. "If you get a ton and a half of wheat per acre in Canada, that's good going," claims Cook. "In Britain, you couldn't make a living with a ton and a half. All land is farmed more intensely in Britain. And there is the moisture—we have a quite a good growing climate."

While the increasing sophistication of machinery and chemicals has changed the character of farming, it is a blessing that the setting remains remarkably unspoiled to the eye. In writing of his boyhood home in Wessex, Thomas Hardy created an image of such familiar detail that even now, 150 years after, it could have been written yesterday:

> It was a small low cottage with a thatched pyramidal roof, and having dormer windows breaking up into the eaves, a single chimney standing in the very midst. The window-shutters were not yet closed, and the fire and candlelight within radiated forth upon the bare boughs of several codlin trees hanging about in various distorted shapes, the result of early

The Cotswolds is an area of rich farmland extending from Chipping Camden in the north to Bath in the south. It forms the watershed between the Thames and the Severn basins.

Houses in the Cotswolds, Oxfordshire, England

training as espaliers, combined with careless climbing into their boughs in later years. The walls of the dwelling were for the most part covered with creepers, though these were rather beaten back from the doorway—a feature which was worn and scratched by much passing in and out, giving it by day the appearance of an old keyhole. Light streamed through the cracks and joints of a wooden shed at the end of the cottage, a sight which nourished a fancy that the purpose of the erection must be rather to veil bright attractions than to shelter unsightly necessities. The noise of a beetle and wedges and the splintering of wood was periodically heard from this direction; and at the other end of the house a steady regular munching and the occasional scurr of a rope betokened a stable, and horses feeding within it.

Owlpen Manor, a Tudor manor house whose origins date to the ninth century, stands in its own remote valley among the South Cotswolds and is the home of Nicholas and Karin Mander.

If there will always be a familiar image of England, it will be that of the rolling downs of the Cotswolds, the fertile limestone hills west of Oxford that form the watershed between the River Thames, which flows east to the North Sea, and the Severn, which flows west to the Bristol Channel and the Irish Sea. These are among the richest agricultural lands in England. The names of Cotswolds villages alone—Chipping Campden, Shipton under Wychwood, and Upper and Lower Slaughter—evoke a sensibility that is as central to the English identity as the works of Shakespeare, who was himself born amid Gloucestershire's "high wild hills and rough uneven ways." While he would make his name in the more cosmopolitan London, it was among the rough country folk that the "Swan of Avon," as Ben Jonson dubbed him, tuned his eyes and ears for the nuances of speech and

114

manner that imbue his characters with such lasting vitality. It was doubtless this land of his youth that he recalled in one rousing and patriotic speech in *Richard II*:

This royal throne of Kings, this sceptered isle,
This earth of majesty, this seat of Mars,
This other Eden, demi-Paradise,
This fortress built by Nature for herself.

Cirencester, a town in the Cotswolds, today has a population of no more than fifteen thousand. In the Roman era, however, Cirencester was England's second-largest town after London, marking the junction of five Roman roads. In the Middle Ages, it was the largest sheep market in all England. But as the English economy moved away from agriculture and focused on industry, this gentle land of rolling hills was largely forgotten. Yet because it was bypassed by the train of progress, the area has managed to preserve its Elizabethan charms—a fact not wasted on the many who visit the area.

Today, sheep continue to play a prominent role in British agriculture. They have never been an unusual sight amid the hills and valleys of England, but as Yorkshire dairyman John Cook observes, today their presence is due more to negative economic forces than before: "We have a lot of upland in England and Wales—the Pennines and the west country—and sheep do better than anything else in those conditions. The lowland farmers in the olden days used to like sheep because they were good for putting fertility into the land—they made for a sort of a break in the rotation between arable crops. But as price pressure has been put on cereals, and particularly as quotas have come onto dairy, the dairy farmers have suddenly found they've got to keep ten less cows this year, so they think, 'I've got some spare land ... Aha! Sheep!'"

Other government interventions are contributing to the preservation of pastoral England. Many farms, like the Cooks', are situated in the midst of national parks where strict laws govern land use. As John Cook explains, "We're part of the North York Moors National Park. There's a lot of moorland when you go back up to the northwest, and there are strict planning controls in this area. If he's not in a national park, a farmer can put up a building without any problem, provided it's less than

Traditional thatched-roof cottages in the Cotswolds

five thousand square feet and provided it's a certain distance from the road. We can't do that here; we have to notify the authorities. We had to turn a building around because they felt it didn't lie right with the hill when they stood at the public viewing point. So we had to turn it until it did. We're going to put up a new shed, and, again, the roof has to be dark brown so it immediately blends in."

Even as the mists lie calm upon these lands, a new problem is emerging. "There's still quite a lot of family farming in Britain," Mr. Cook says. "But we've had strange economics, because all these insurance companies came into agriculture in the seventies in quite a big way. The land's gone their way, and they're all busy selling up and pulling out now. Their place is being taken over by people who have been made rich in the financial boom that occurred in the eighties. These people are buying the land, but they don't want to farm it themselves. They've got jobs in London or other big cities. They live in the main house, probably renting the land to neighboring farmers to farm it. So we're seeing the landlord-tenant system starting again."

Beyond whatever other distinctions of class there might be among the farming population as a whole, John Cook's wife sees two types of farmer: the full-timer and the part-timer. She wonders what impact the city-bred sophisticates with no ties to the land will have on rural England: "A few years ago, there were people coming

A gypsy cart and pony

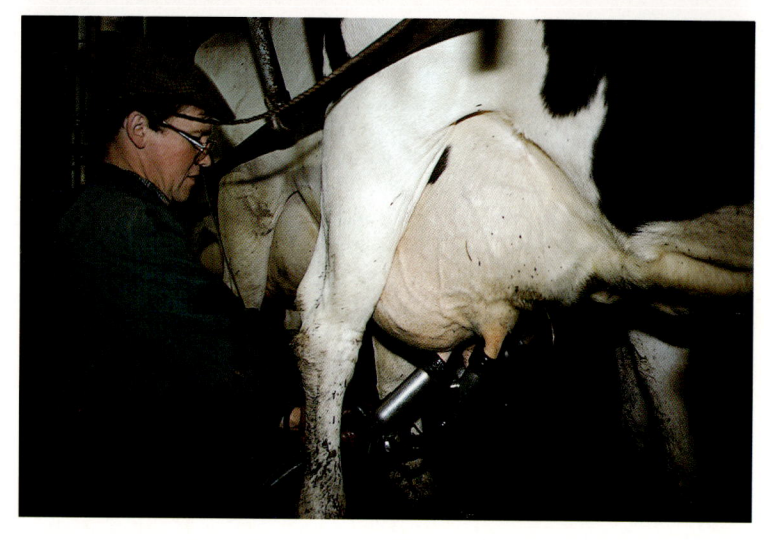

The farm and family of dairy farmer John Cook, located in North Yorkshire

OVERLEAF: *Yorkshire farmland*

into the countryside who physically wanted to join in the rural way of life. They're becoming less now. They are being replaced by an urban middle class who want to live in the country, people who are very well off—doctors, dentists, managing directors. The idea is to buy a nice farmhouse with a hundred acres and have a few beasts on it. They're living in a nice place, and they can easily afford to commute the few miles every day. What happens is that the rural community that exists disappears. In this area we're already seeing a two-class sort of structure. We're getting people who work in Scarborough; they farm only part-time, and they have no involvement with the local community at all. The rural communities are being slowly destroyed because the people who come in have totally different values. This is happening all over England."

A Hampshire farmer recalls, "Oh, the memories of a most peaceful place, the village community. Everyone knew everyone. It was a happy and a friendly community. If you lived on a farm, there was never a dull moment. There was always something going on—shearing or sheep dipping or cows coming in for milking, animals going to market or new animals coming in, corn being cut or harvesting . . . never a dull moment if you lived in a village farming community."

It is possible that the winds of change are beginning to swing again in favor of the farmer and that the benefit will also accrue to the nation as a whole. John Cook explains: "Like all other farmers, we like what we're doing and wouldn't change it for anything, but there's a lot of worry that we're going to be the last of a line, that the children just won't be able to take over the farm—in part because farms today just aren't large enough. The profitability tends to come down in real terms per acre, and there just isn't enough surface left over to farm it and make a living. We're seeing people going out. So to that extent, we're the same as the rest of the world, unless we have a significant greening of governments and the European Economic Community—particularly if they want to pump money in to keep people in the countryside. In the national park, for example, they're trying to get money to pay farmers who are prepared to farm at a much lower level; they'll give income aid to those who are willing to farm traditionally. That will keep people in the countryside, and we're going to see it being done on larger and larger farms."

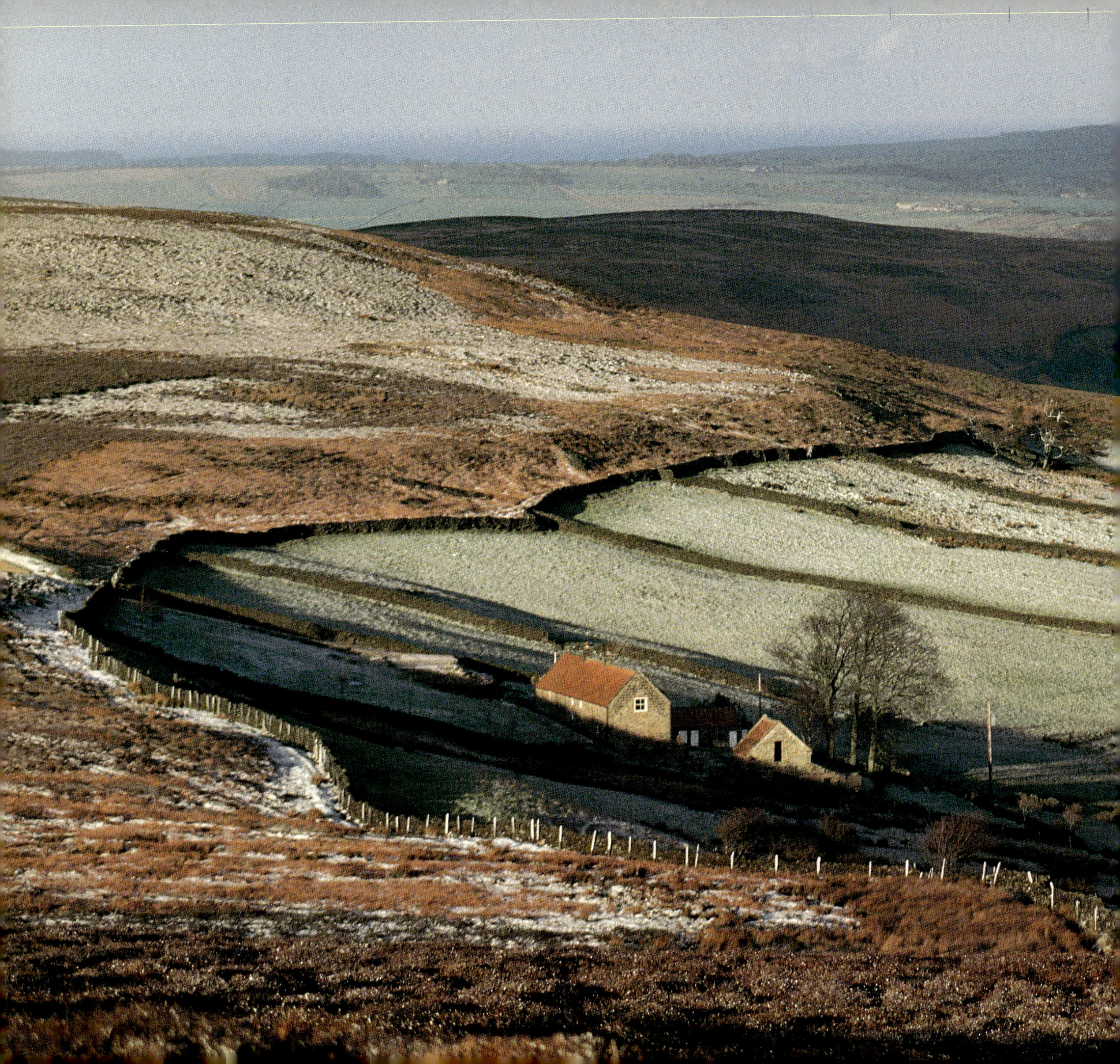

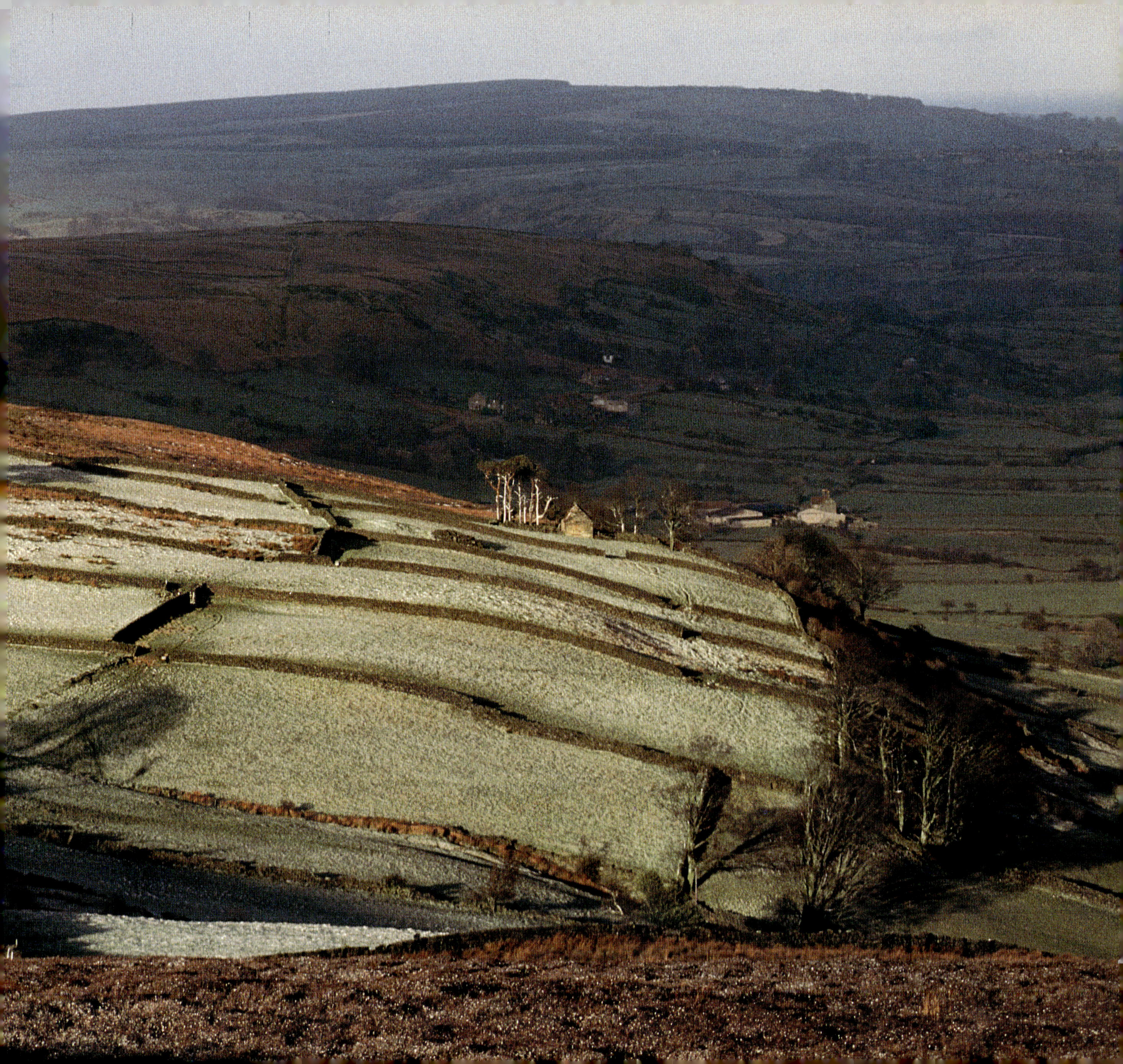

Yorkshire Moor

A sudden spring snowstorm on the North Yorkshire Moor

North Yorkshire Moors

The city of York

York Minster Cathedral, England's largest cathedral

Scarborough, located on the eastern coast of North Yorkshire county, is a popular resort known as the "Queen of the Yorkshire Coast."

Scarborough

OPPOSITE: *A coal-fired electric power plant in northern England*

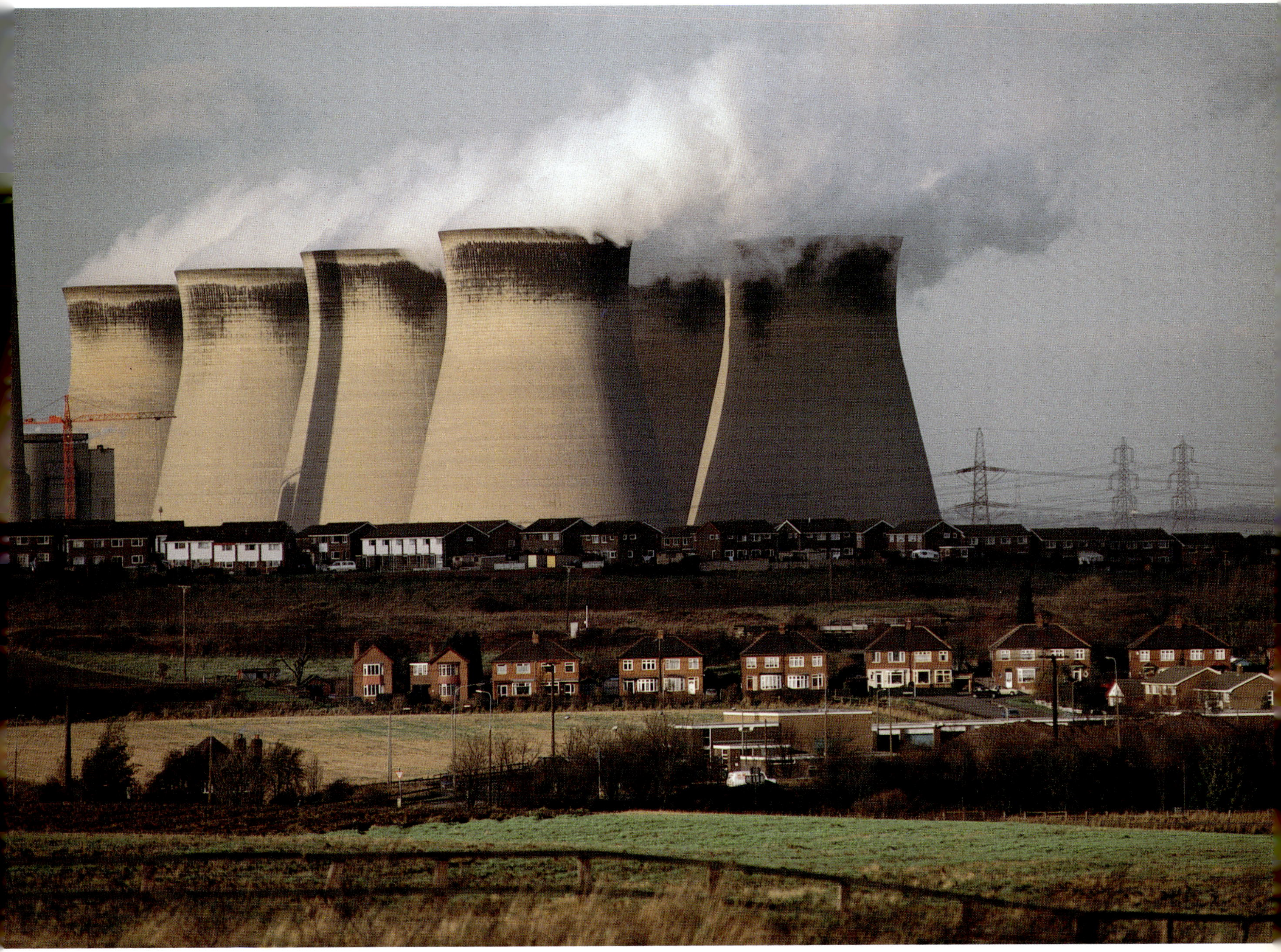

The colliery in Easington, a mining town on England's northeast coast

OPPOSITE LEFT: *With almost no prospects for employment, the youth of Easington have little more to do than hang out.*

OPPOSITE RIGHT: *Easington teenager*

Easington

The farther north one goes in England, the bleaker the landscape becomes. In the northeast corner around Newcastle, the coal-mining industry, for which the region is famous, is being threatened with extinction. When it goes, so, too, will whole towns and communities that grew up around the pits, where mining has been a way of life passed down from father to son over generations. The village of Easington, once a thriving town on the North Sea south of Newcastle, now faces a future as dark as a stormy winter's sky. Since the devastating miners' strike of 1984, the pit has been threatened with closure.

"There is no future in Easington, as far as I'm concerned, and as far as all of us are concerned," says one man who lives in the town. "It's a dying community. I could see this pit closing in five years, and there'll be no one living here except maybe retired people. There's no hope: no jobs, no hope."

Also lost is the sense of community or common purpose that used to sustain the mining families of Easington and countless similar villages. "Folks from other places say, 'Aw, it's just a pit; they're just closing a factory down.' It's not the same," explains Heather Wood, a mother of two. "It's bad closing a factory, but closing a pit's different. That pit's our community. Years ago, they used to say they built the community around the church; here they built it around the pit."

The livelihood that coal mining provided for Easington's residents has always been dangerous. Sudden explosions and collapsing shafts have claimed thousands of lives and crippled countless others. One such tragedy is eloquently described in an Easington folk song:

*Come listen all ye miner lads that tack the road in by,
And I will tell a tragic tale when ten times eight did die.
At Easington in '51, they saw the gates of hell.
But they that lived to see the sight, they did not live to tell.*

*The day, the 29th of May, a tragic trick of fate,
Found the night shift and the fore shift in the gate.
Explosion wrecked the quarter seam and killed them all but one,
And many a miner's humble home lost father, brother, son.*

*'Twas fire, damp beneath the cut, coal dust fed the flame
That wrought out till it was spent, then roared in by again.
Tearing, twisting roads apart from their truly bed
And left behind our sorrow with the dying and the dead.*

*Within the hour from Howden Lea the rescue team did come,
With them, hope, to find the blind and listen to the dumb.
But hope was killed by after damp, by gas we miners dread.
Two rescue men with yellow birds were numbered with the
   dead.*

The mines have taken their toll in the form of black-lung disease. "Me son's grandfather worked down in the pit forty years," Heather relates. "He's retired now with emphysema. He can't breathe. I mean, that's what gets me. You can work down the mine all your working life, and you can give your all. When I was small, I can remember the colliery calling me dad in to say, 'What a good job you've done, you've worked hard.' And then when me dad had an accident and couldn't work down the pit anymore, they couldn't find him a job. That was his reward for working, for giving his life. That's what he's done. The disease was caused by mining, and now he's so ill that he's given his life!"

Ironically, the people of Easington both fear and defend the dangerous pits. "As much as we all hate the pit, you see, that's the only thing we've got," explains Heather. "We fought to keep our pit, but at the same time we all hate the pit because it gives us a sense of fear. But if it's the only thing, then you opt for it."

The youth, in particular, are losing hope fast. Their days are spent in a seemingly endless limbo. "Years ago in Easington," continues Heather, "I had an elderly uncle. He'd never married, so he used to take our family out. I can remember he used to take us to the seats where

Neil Patrick Shaw, a miner in Bagville

OPPOSITE LEFT: *A retired coal miner at the Easington colliery club*

OPPOSITE RIGHT: *Another retired miner who began work at the age of 14*

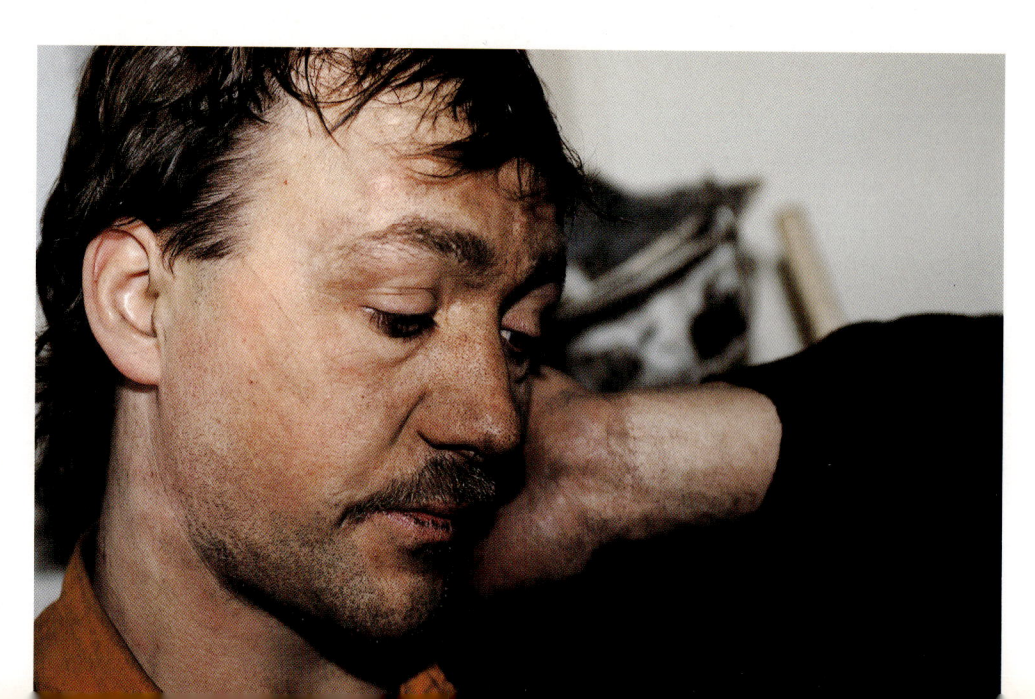

Marilyn, another Easington resident, agrees: "They just walk the streets, buying pop and crisps and sandwiches. Just to be out rather than sit in the house getting depressed."

Some youngsters drink to escape the boredom of their daily lives. "Sure, I go out drinking," says one. "Drinking's all there is to do. Day after day, walking down the streets, sitting on the seats, and that's it."

Fortunately, not everyone is without hope or the determination to succeed. John Hall, a third-generation miner from north of Newcastle, is a self-made man and a successful developer. He lives in Winyard Hall, an estate

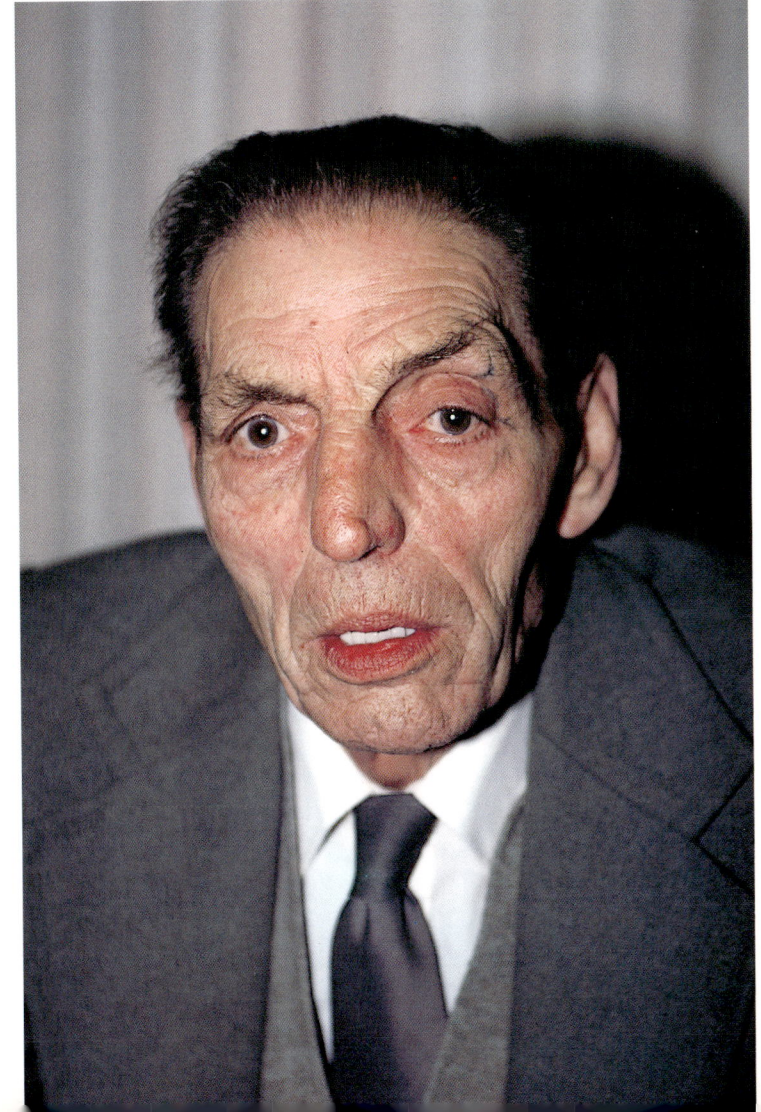

the old men sat and tell us stories. Now there are still elderly men about, but it's mainly young people. Years ago, it was those who'd left work; now it's those who cannot find any work, and that's all they've got to do, stand about. And we can't provide anything else because we haven't got the money to provide it.

"It hurts to look at young people, because I can see that they think 'What does anybody care about me?' When you talk to them, certainly, that's what they say to you: 'What are you going to do for me? What's the older generation think of us? They're not doing very much for us.'"

John Hall

RIGHT: *The shopping mall built by John Hall, near Newcastle*

134

that belonged to the Third Marquis of Londonderry, once one of the richest and most powerful men in England. He was a man, says Hall, "I'd always been taught to think of as the enemy—the mine owner who in many ways did nothing to give us work, did nothing socially for my particular section of the community."

Hall made his fortune in real estate, but his crowning achievement is the construction of Newcastle's Metro Center, which represents Hall's conscious effort to recreate the small-town sense of community that he knew in poverty as a child.

"My dream started over forty years ago, I suppose, in my mining town where I used to live. The town had a high street—a lot of shops, a cinema, the ice cream parlors, and the church. It was a place where my parents used to take me on a Saturday, sometimes Sunday, and we used to meet our friends there. It was for more than shopping. It was a getting together of people. And this is what I've done here. You don't have to spend a dollar here. You can come down to the Metro Center and just sit and watch the world go by.

"With the Metro Center, I try to reflect many of the social changes that are happening in our society today. Even though people have a lot more money, there are still a lot of lonely people. We've tried to cater to the disabled, to the blind. It's a place where you can come enjoy life, and most people do. It's my roots, really. I've tried to reflect what we are in the northeast, what a great family, a community."

A woman describes the value the shopping center holds for the neighborhood: "The Metro Center took seven years to come to fruition. And I can honestly say that the dream John Hall created for this northern region actually came true. He had a vision of his mining village under glass—more than just shopping. People could meet their friends. Lonely people could come. And everything he dreamed is in that shopping center now."

Hall is greatly admired by his neighbors. As one re-

Easington greenhouses—plots of unused land that are rented to people who grow flowers and vegetables.

tired miner put it, "I can't really explain the way I feel about him. I admire the man, living in a little coal-mining village like a plant and sprouting up like a huge, magnificent tree."

John Hall is excited about the future. For him, the closing of the mines presents the people of the northeast with a challenge to overcome great odds: "We've been forced to the negotiating table in many ways. And the Prime Minister, Mrs. Thatcher, has realized, in a sense, that we have to change and that she had to make people realize that change was necessary to the U.K. Her work has been in giving a sense of individual ambition and responsibility to ordinary people and saying to them, you can do whatever you want to do.

"It's a totally new spirit in the U.K. In this area of the northeast, which is one of the old industrial areas, I've never known anything like it. There's a climate of enterprise. Profit's no longer a dirty word. I believe we're un-

Houses in Easington—the boarded windows reflect the hard times befallen the town's mineworkers.

OPPOSITE: *Residents of Easington often scour the beach for coal that has fallen and washed ashore from barges docked at the nearby colliery.*

dergoing a social revolution as important as the industrial revolution, and it's changing the whole atmosphere of our thinking and our culture. Nobody really knows where we're going. It's an exciting time."

Few Easington residents share Hall's enthusiasm for the future. "I would never encourage anybody to live around here," says one Easington woman. "Some probably like coming here because it's old-fashioned and, you know, it's quiet and all that. But there's no chance, no opportunities here, no jobs or anything. People say there is, but they haven't tried getting jobs. We know because we live here, and there is not anything here."

Edinburgh Castle has been, in its time, not merely a fortress, but a palace, a treasury, the home of the national records, a workshop and a storehouse for munitions.

Scotland

It is still and breathless, but overhead is just the faintest smothered flush in the greyness, a promise that the sun will break through in his due time. Then, imperceptibly at first, begins one of the most beautiful atmospheric phenomena in the British Isles. Vague shapes are seen in the mist, or rather you imagine them from a hint here and there of far-off shadows. You realize that something tremendous is hiding there in the immense impenetrability. The mist thins in patches, and again comes that shadow of a shadow, as though some mighty Armada is lying becalmed at anchor in the grey sea.

But the shapes in the mist are not masts and crosstrees. Bit by bit an unbelievable vision uplifts itself, at first like a mirage which hangs uncertain in the air over a desert, and then, etched in toneless grey, as if painted in thin smoke against the sky, a phantom city emerges spire by spire, pinnacle by pinnacle, tower by tower: a ghostly city on the edge of a steep ravine: a Camelot, a Tintagel; a city turreted and loopholed; a city that seems to spring from the mist to the sound of horns; a city that seems still to grasp a sword.

So old Edinburgh looks down in these autumn mornings over a grey mist, and over many centuries, to New Edinburgh.

—H. V. MORTON (1892–1979),
IN SEARCH OF SCOTLAND

Calton Hill Cemetary overlooking Old Edinburgh

Scotland, no less than Wales or Northern Ireland, is a land rich in history, folklore, and song. Such items of apparel as the tartan kilt, the trews, and the doublet and hose are emblems of a Scottish individuality—a pride that often finds expression in some very strong words. "I'm very much a Scottish patriot," states Bob Brinkman, a Scots Highlander. "We don't like being ruled by Westminster. They simply forget that we are a nation with our own identity. Westminster treats us not as second-class citizens but third-class."

It appears to be common for the people of the countries of Great Britain to protect fiercely their sense of a separate identity. One might even suggest that this feeling of self-worth has been the cornerstone of Britain's endurance. This is not to suggest that the English haven't tried to suppress the identities of their subjects. At one point, following the crushing victory of the English over Bonnie Prince Charlie at Culloden Moor in 1746, the tartan dress was actually forbidden by an Act of Parliament. Such restrictions, however, clearly did more to enliven the spirit of the Scots than to quell it. Says Brinkman, "Great Britain is one place, but it's made up of four different nations—not just countries but nations!"

The Highlands is a brooding and beautiful mountain-

A taxi stand in Edinburgh

RIGHT: *A street performer outside the National Gallery of Scotland, in Edinburgh*

The Firth of Forth, Scotland

Tiny fishing villages dot the coast along the north side of the Firth of Forth.

143

ous region in northern Scotland. The land is tough and the living poor, helping to explain a certain tightness associated with the Scottish. The character of the Scot is most clearly defined in the Highlander—a fighter quick to take offense, honor-bound, and a patriot. The Highlands is also the country of the clans—MacKenzies, MacDonalds, Camerons, and Fletchers. The English sense of social hierarchy is contrasted in these clans, where every man is part of a *family,* no matter how far removed from them. It was once said: "Scotsmen are clannish—touch one and you touch all."

While feisty and quick-tempered, the Scot nonetheless has a soft side, which is characterized by a great warmth and generosity of soul—features undoubtedly cultivated

Elie, Scotland's east coast

144

Forth River, Scotland

by the strong sense of family. The Scot is also as prone as the Welshman to indulge in song and celebration, a tendency that helps counteract the tougher aspects of life in the Highlands.

One of the more unfortunate trends in Scottish history has been the desertion of its people, sometimes by forceful means, often for lack of opportunity. In the eighteenth century, sheep, and then deer, were seen to be more profitable tenants than the crofters, who were evicted and sent away to distant lands. In the nineteenth century, the industrial revolution drew thousands away from the country in search of jobs in the big cities. Even today, anyone with even a whisper of ambition has little choice but to migrate to commercial centers like London. Those who leave Scotland's pastures of purple heather

The Scottish Highlands

RIGHT: *Rannoch Moor, Highlands*

OPPOSITE: *Castle Stalker, located on a small island in Loch Creran*

usually find the attraction to their homeland intensified. Lucinda Sieger, now settled in London, often feels the tug of her Scottish heartstrings. "When I came down from Scotland to pursue a career in the arts," she recalls, "I found a huge difference between the Scots and the English. The difference in human warmth is incredible. I've been in London for eleven years, and the doors are always shut. So when I'm feeling lost and in need of support, I really feel like going back to Scotland and recharging the batteries by just getting out in the fresh air and seeing family. There's just great support in Scotland. I feel the people are ready to receive you. They want to talk. They're much more approachable, and they're very open. You know what they're wanting."

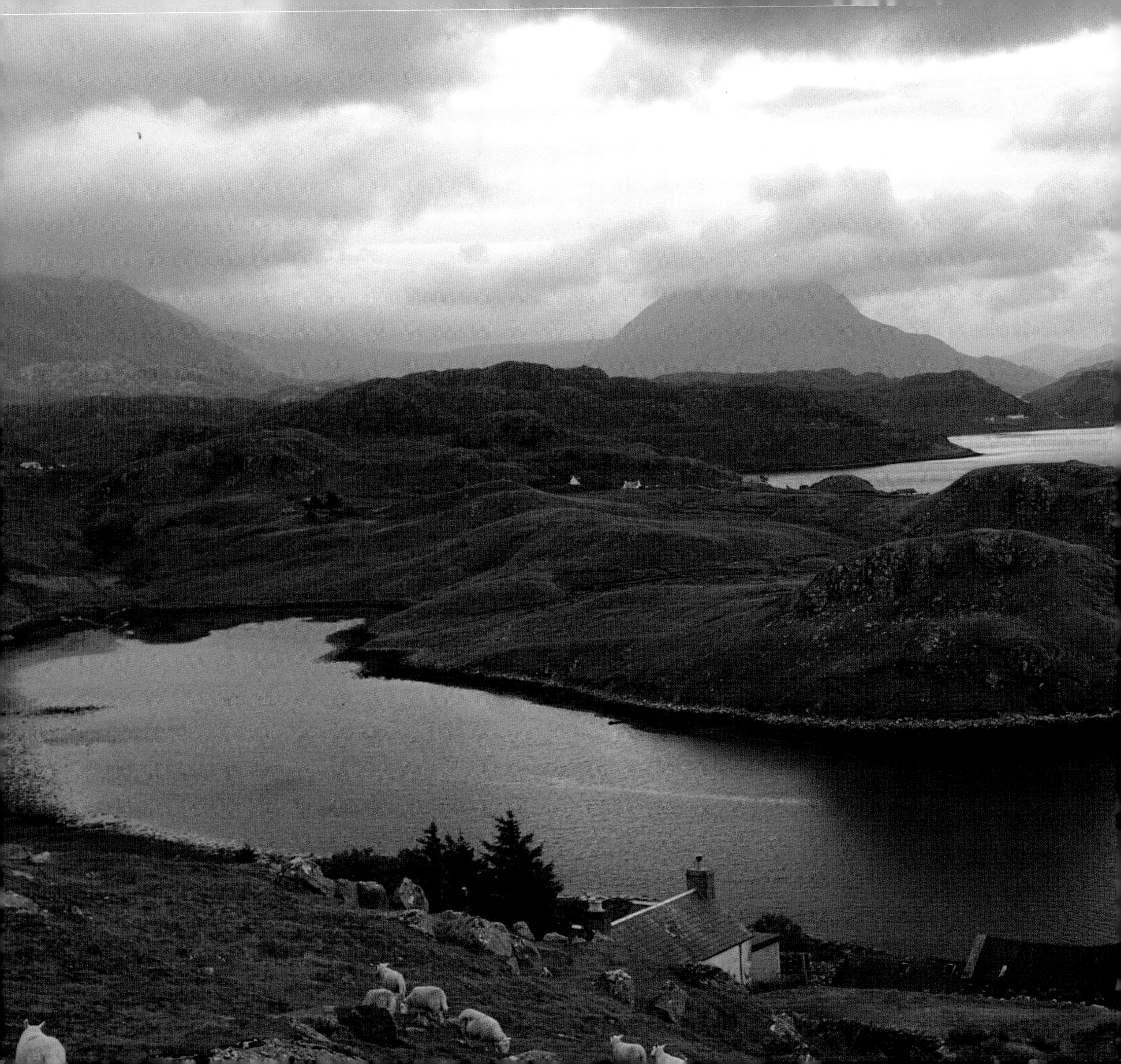

Near Cape Wrath, Scottish Highlands. A Norse word meaning "turning point," Wrath is where the ships turned south.

OVERLEAF: *The landscape surrounding Cape Wrath*

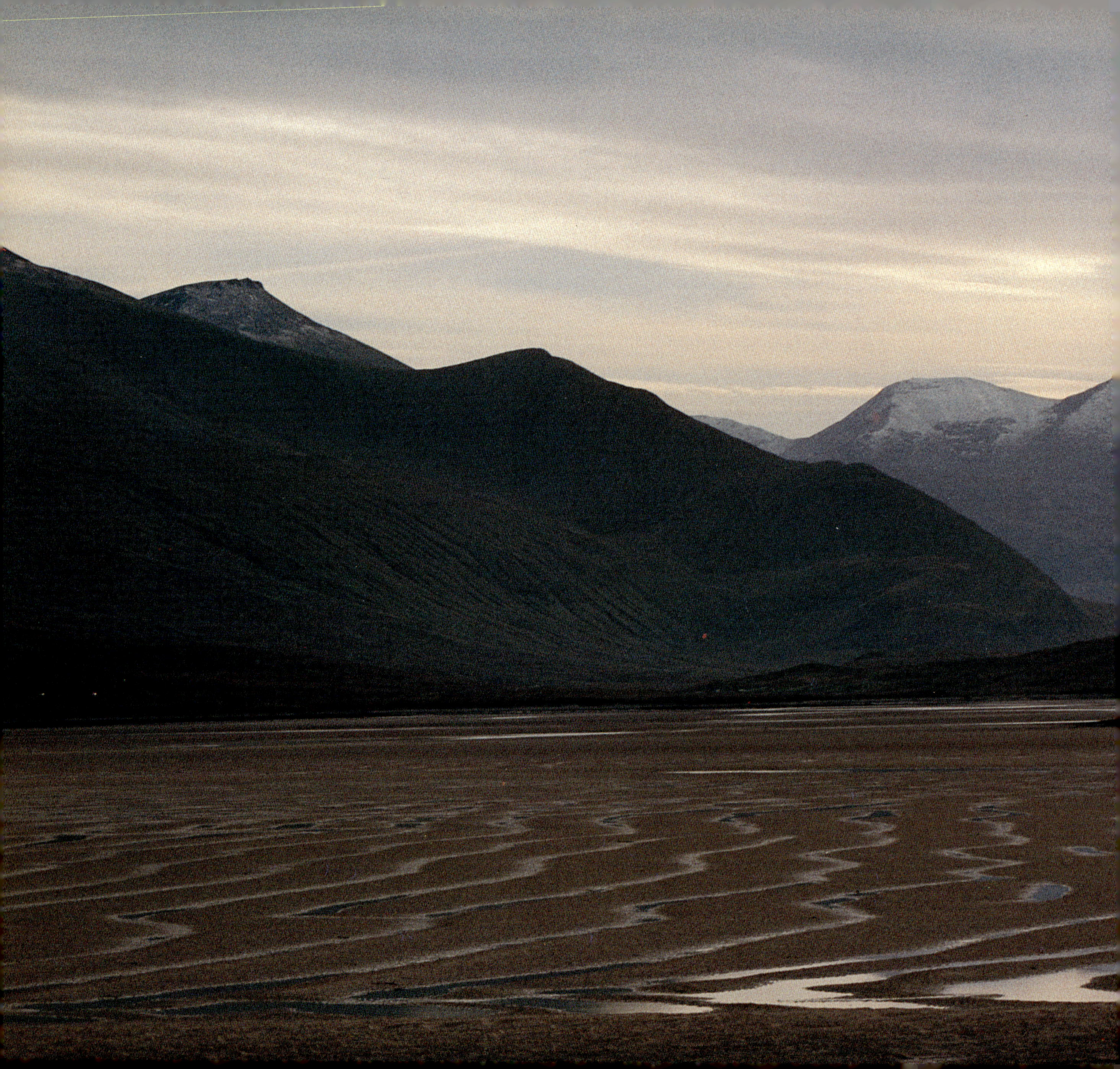

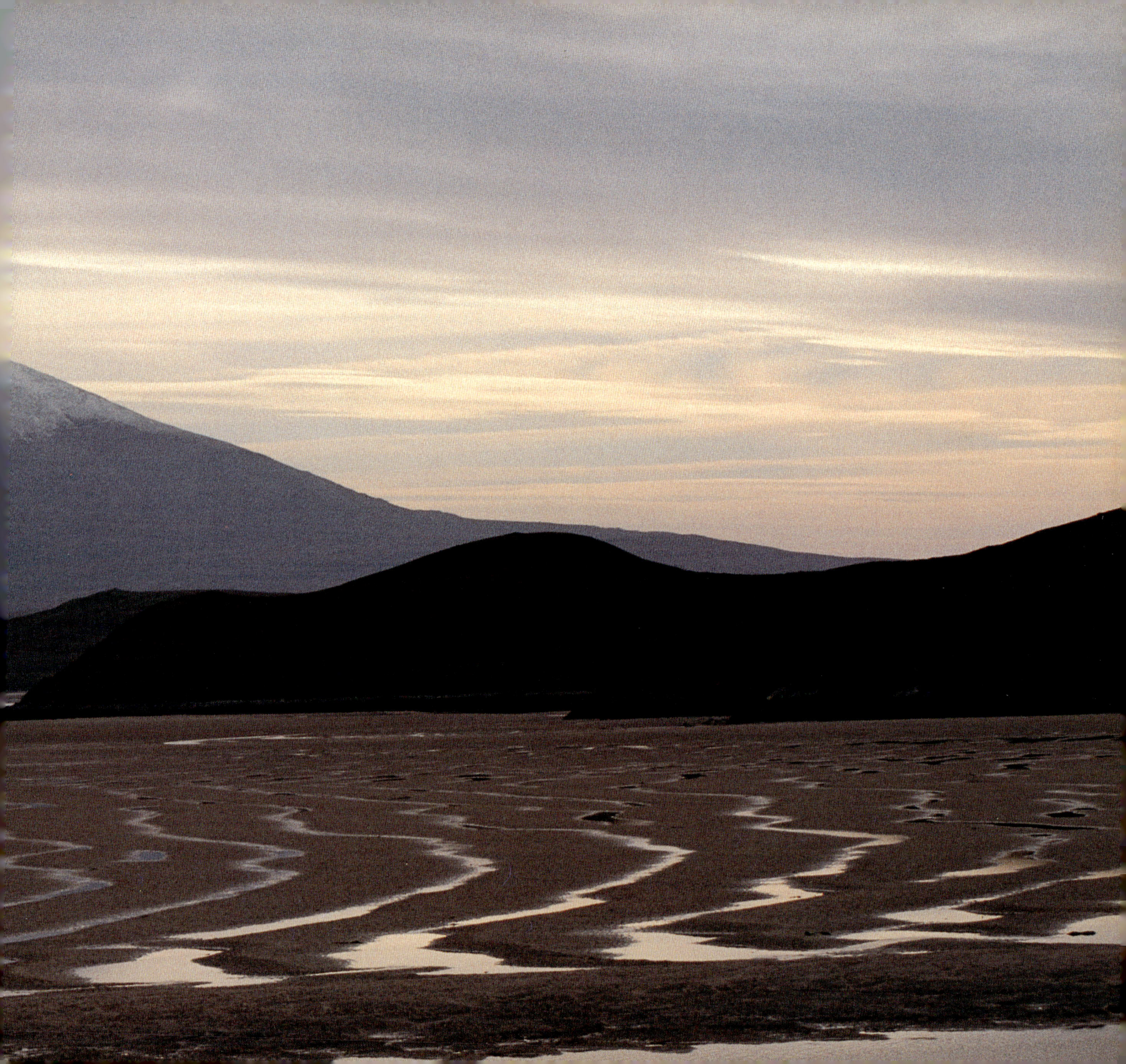

Glencoe

If there is one particular event in Scottish history that never fails to boil the blood and inspire the clannish warrior in the Scot, it might very well be the Massacre of Glencoe, also know as the glen of weeping. Here, in 1691, thirty-eight men, women, and children of the MacDonald clan were brutally murdered by a regiment of soldiers—all Campbells and hereditary enemies of the MacDonalds—acting under orders from King William III, who had been misled into believing the MacDonalds had refused to pledge an oath of allegiance. While Highland history is full of examples of barbaric acts between clans, Glencoe is particularly remembered. The Campbells marched in, expressed friendship for the MacDonalds, and were received with traditional Highland hospitality. At the given signal, they turned on their hosts and slew them, one and all. Such desperate acts of treachery are not easily forgotten, or forgiven.

Adding to this dark memory is the landscape of Glencoe itself, which is dominated by great, slashing rocks and deep, haunting shadows. Charles Dickens, in a little-known letter, described passing through Glencoe:

> Glencoe itself is perfectly terrible. The pass is an awful place. It is shut in on each side by enormous rocks from which great torrents come rushing down in all directions. In amongst these rocks on one side of the pass (the left as we came) there are scores of glens, high up, which form such haunts as you might imagine yourself wandering in, in the very height and madness of a fever. They will live in my dreams for years—I was going to say as long as I live, and I seriously think so. The very recollection of them makes me shudder...

Is it the ghosts of the MacDonalds living in the haunting glens that made such an impression on Dickens? In a land known for its folklore, its legends shrouded in mist, its history of battles, it would not be hard to mistake momentary fears for overwhelming sensations of dread. "I suppose," wrote H. V. Morton, "everyone who has been alone in mist on mountains or in lonely places has felt at some time that queer panic which causes a man to turn and look behind him. It is almost as if an invisible presence were at one's elbow and might at any moment reveal itself. It is not difficult to realize why the ancients gave each hill and stream its guardian spirit."

Glencoe, "the glen of weeping"

Isle of Lewis

Of all the countries of the British Isles, Scotland has the most geographical and cultural divisions: the Highlands, the Lowlands, the Orkney and Shetland Islands, and the Outer Hebrides, which is part of the Western Islands and separated from the mainland by a body of water called the Minch.

The Isle of Lewis is the largest and northernmost of the Hebrides. Its natural harbors have made Lewis an ideal haven for fishing boats. Remote and desolate, the Isle of Lewis is home for a few hundred hardy souls. Robin Mirrlees, a veteran of the British Empire, explains how he came to live there:

"I saw it advertised in a magazine, and I thought, 'What fun!' I came up here a bit unprepared. As a matter of fact, I sent the check without actually coming to see it. I thought if I did, my trustees would twist my arm and stop me coming. Anyway, I'm glad I did.

"Although this is a small island, you can find every type of life here. You find funny people and sad people, intelligent people and very brave people. For a couple of thousand years, they had to fight to survive here, risking their lives deep-sea fishing. Practically every family here has some tragedy. They've probably lost a son or a brother, because deep-sea fishing is very dangerous. But it's very rewarding, very creative.

"The land here is bleak and doesn't produce much. The great wealth lies in the sea. Recently—in the last ten years—salmon fishing has been developed, and I think this is proving very successful.

"It's a hard life, but I wish I'd had the first half of my life here. It would have been very good training.

"The reward I get today is living here with some very remarkable people who've had to fight their way. This has made some of them rather tough, a little bit unfeeling, but, nevertheless, I admire them."

Life on this island has changed since Mirrlees first ar-

Fisherman from the Butt of Lewis, the northern-most point on the Isle of Lewis, Outer Hebrides

Peat being laid out to dry on the Isle of Lewis. The slow-burning peat is used primarily to heat homes.

rived. "When I first came here, many years ago," he explains, "people called on one another a lot. That's slightly dying out; people are beginning to lead a more hectic way of life. They're trying to grab the goodies of this world and build up rapid fortunes. And so they don't have much time to enjoy themselves or their neighbors the way they used to.

"Gaelic is still spoken in the family by middle-age people or older. There's plenty of ninety-eight- and ninety-nine-year-old people here. Young people, eighteen years old, have left. We've kept the Gaelic form from dying out. It reminds me of an old proverb that you don't really know how much you love anybody or appreciate a thing until the day you lose it."

Doune Carloway Village with the broch in the background

LEFT: *Dun Carloway Broch, Isle of Lewis*

The Standing Stones of Callanish

The most notable feature on the Isle of Lewis is the Standing Stones of Callanish. As with Stonehenge in England, the meaning behind these neolithic standing stones is unknown. They speak to modern man on an individual basis.

"When you first come to Callanish," explains Robin Mirrlees, "from a distance you get this mystic feeling, and the closer you get, the vibrations get stronger and stronger. No man can stay unmoved as he walks slowly up the avenue towards these stones. In Gaelic, one of their names is 'the false men of Callanish,' meaning that when you see them from a distance they look like a procession of men with cloaks over their heads walking up the hill. You get the same feeling, if not stronger, that you get inside a great European cathedral.

"Some people say that when you put your ear on the stones, you can hear them breathing inside. The fact is they've got such powerful vibrations that they've given rise to many myths and legends. They are nearly four thousand years old, people say; certainly three thousand years old—from a time when most of Europe was totally undeveloped and uncivilized.

"So I come here and meditate. I feel that, at the moment, the Western world is going through a terrible period of chaos. It reminds me of the Reformation and the Counter Reformation. Perhaps we are on the verge of some new philosophy; perhaps some new religion will evolve out of all this chaos. Or perhaps, in a hundred years' time, somebody or something will come along and solve all our problems. This is where I come to think it over.

"In a small-scale, different sort of way, this rather reminds me of the disappearance of the British Empire. It must have required a considerable amount of sub-strata of culture and human energy to erect these stones, to bring them along. There must have been a well established religion or culture for many thousands of years. Now it's vanished; not a trace remains. We can't prove it. The most learned professors and archaeologists have tried to find out what this culture was all about. It's vanished. And will the British Empire completely vanish from the memory of our descendants? I don't know. I think it's a pity if it does."

Standing Stones of Callanish—the finest stone circle in Scotland

Finhorn Bay, northeast coast of Scotland

Foula

The tiny island of Foula lies roughly fourteen miles off the west coast of the Shetland Islands, the northernmost of the British Isles. The Shetlands, a sort of island barrier between the North Sea and the Atlantic Ocean, are the only fixed points between the clashing forces of wind and sea. The Romans came this far two thousand years ago and called it *Ultima Thule,* the "end of the world."

Given their proximity to Norway two hundred miles to the east, it is not surprising that the Shetlands were among the earliest lands in what is now British territory to fall under the control of the Vikings. "It wouldn't have been remote at that time," says Foula inhabitant John Holbourn. "It would have been one of the most accessible places then, when all world travel was done by sea. It was very difficult to travel over land. Shetland was a crossroads at one time; it's where civilizations crossed."

Six centuries of Norse rule had a considerable impact, particularly on Foula, where a Norse dialect continued to be spoken until the nineteenth century. As John Holbourn's wife, Isobel, observes, "All over the island you'll find traces of the Norse words."

The first historical inhabitants of Foula seem to have been swept there on the tide of Christianity. "It was the first of the Christian movement, coming up from from Iona and Ireland and the west coast of Scotland," explains Isobel. "They must have reached here maybe two or three hundred years after they first settled Iona. Old Dutch maps from about 1600 show all the islands: the mainland of Shetland is just sort of a mass, but the outside islands were obviously the staging points. The island of Papa Stour is very near Foula, and Papa Stour means 'big priest.'"

In Foula, magnificent cliffs rear more than twelve hundred feet high and provide sanctuary for tens of thousands of birds but only a few hundred people. Rugged and forbidding, the wind-swept island makes for rough

PAGES 161, 162: *Foula Isle, part of Scotland's Shetland Islands. Foula is really only half an island—its west side having been cut away as though sliced by a giant's knife, leaving a sheer rampart of cliff rising as high as 1,300 feet.*

living in the storm-wracked North Sea, but according to Isobel, it also defines its people: "I think the history and character of the island make the people what they are. If the people are strong, independent people, then it's because of the heritage of the island and how these little things build up.

"An island is a geographical area that is clearly defined. It doesn't have a border that is simply a line on a map. You have to cross the sea to get to it, so anything that comes in has to make quite a big impression before it can alter the way of life. I think that's been the case in Foula and possibly in Britain. Because of its insularity, it's maintained its distinctive qualities. And being a maritime nation, being near to the sea, helps to give you character as well."

This character is manifest in the children of Foula. Because the population numbers only in the hundreds, there is no school on the island. At a very early age, the children are sent for their education to Lerwick, the capital of

Shetland ponies on Foula Isle

Frank Millsopp, who lives on Foula, with daughter Katie

Isobel Holbourn of Foula

OPPOSITE: *John and Isobel Holbourn, owners of Foula Isle.*

Shetland. "The Foula children always come into school with a very strong sense of identity," says Isobel. "They have a very strong sense of being important in the community, with their little jobs and their little part to play. They grow up with a feeling of confidence and belonging, which gives them quite a good start in life. They have a certain amount of confidence not found in children without that kind of upbringing."

Mainlanders often regard islanders as insular, but as John Holbourn explains, "A claustrophobic, introspective feeling was balanced by the fact that the greater part of the men went away to sea. A lot of them sailed all over the world or went to the Antarctic or whaling. It made Foula a lot more cosmopolitan than you'd ever imagine a remote island could be."

At the same time, though, development on the island was remarkably slow. "The first wheel only came to Foula this century," jokes Mr. Holbourn. "I mean, that's the sort of leap the place has taken. It's always interested me very greatly: there were those men traveling the world, seeing everything happening, but the way of life here just didn't change.

"The people of Foula really clung to the old way of life, because there weren't really many outside influences to change it. About twenty years ago, it was quite common for the island to be without a boat for, say, eight weeks at a time. Certain items of foodstuff would go short, and the newspapers would report that Foula Isle was cut off for eight weeks and that we were short of food and this kind of thing.

"That doesn't happen much any more because communications are so good. Also, people are better off and better able to store food. People didn't have much money in the early sixties, and storing large quantities of food was difficult. Conditions are a lot easier for all of us now."

Although their lifestyle is quite primitive by modern standards, John and Isobel Holbourn never think about leaving, especially not after the long, hard journey that brought them to Foula in the first place. John recalls: "My earliest memory is of the boat trip into Foula. I was just five years old at the time, and the boat was an open boat then; it had no deck. To keep warm, I was tucked underneath the tarpaulin that was covering the boxes, with just my head sticking out. I was lying up in the bow of the boat, and there were splits in the boards—she was a very old boat—and I could see the sky out through this crack. Every now and again, the boat would come down in the water, and a spear of water would come in on my face. And that's one of my first memories of the trip to Foula."

"One thing living here has taught me is to take each day as it comes," says Penelope Millsopp, another islander. "It's given me the strength of character I didn't have before; it's made me very patient and very tolerant. The weather dictates what happens and when it happens. This makes you very responsive to the weather and very dependent upon it. If something doesn't happen, nothing's going to make it happen, and you have to learn to live with it."

"I certainly wouldn't be the person I am now if I hadn't lived here," agrees Isobel Holbourn. "I've learned how to tackle things that I never would have dreamt of. I've learned how to cope with death at very close quarters, which is not an easy thing to do at any time. Islanders have to bury their own dead. It's a very basic ceremony. Someone will make the coffin, the nearest neighbors will comfort the family. But here, you get a strength because it is a community.

"What makes people like us want to live here is a very difficult question to answer. It's either a multitude of things or it's a very deep love and identification and loyalty to the place. It's a passionate attachment, really.

"The light in Foula is actually what makes it for me—the sky and the sea and the light that changes all the time with different kinds of weather. I've been in Foula now for nearly thirty years, and I can still gasp at the light effects. It's quite remarkable, the variety. You just gasp with wonder at the beauty. And the sea's so mobile, especially on a windy day, that you get shafts of sunlight catching everything.

"Many different people from different walks of life feel the same things here. It's very difficult to describe. You really have to experience it to know what it's all about. People can come here for twenty-four hours and feel it or be here a month and go away unmoved. But if it hits you, it hits you hard. People come back year after year for the holidays, simply because they say that Foula withdrawal is too painful."

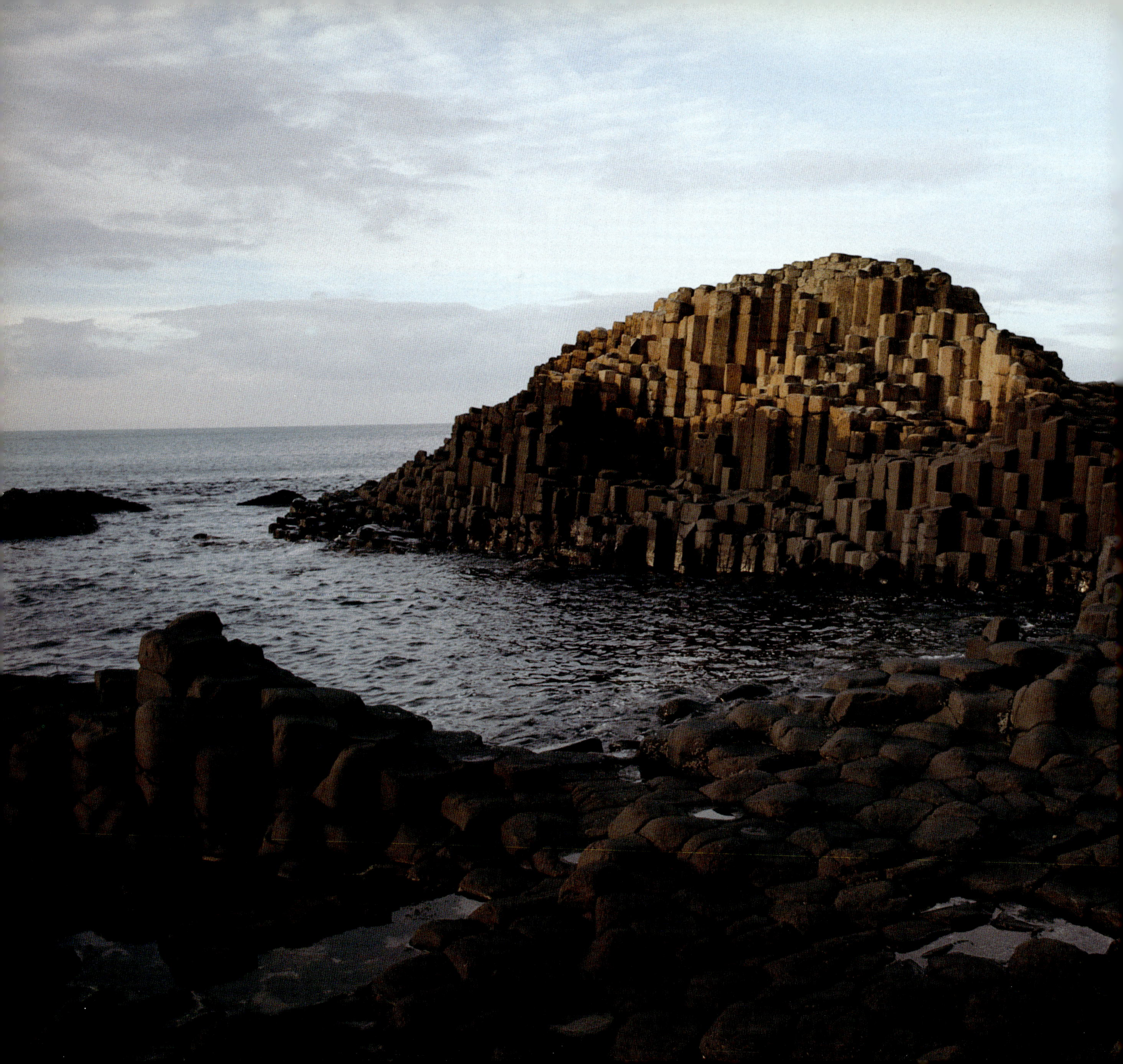

NORTHERN IRELAND

PAGES 166-168: *Giant's Causeway, Northern Ireland's Antrim Coast*

OPPOSITE: *Dunluce Castle, a ruined castle near Giant's Causeway*

Northern Ireland

"You have to be born in Northern Ireland to understand it," says Father Alec Reid, one of Belfast's most respected priests. "It would be a wee bit out of place for an Irishman like me to be in a book about the British." Nonetheless, Reid and others have provided their words and allowed their photographs to be taken in the hope of addressing some of the complexities surrounding this troubled province. One hundred years ago, Northern Ireland—popularly known as Ulster—was part of Ireland. Britain partitioned the country in 1920, institutionalizing the privileged position of the Protestant majority in the north.

Much of Ulster's rich farmland was settled by Scots, ancestors of Presbyterian Reverend Brian Moore, who explains that "in the north, the people with big estates are generally Protestants. Their families go back hundreds of years." Father Paddy O'Donnell, who was born in the north, agrees with Reverend Moore but adds: "In 1898, most Presbyterians were for a united Ireland. The nineteenth century had seen a wave of anti-Catholic sentiment in reaction to the smoldering anger of those Catholics who were dispossessed of their lands in Ulster. All the good land wound up with the Protestants and the boggy land with the Catholics. The then-Unionists were supported by the conservative Randolph Churchill, who said, 'Home Rule is Rome Rule.' He didn't give a damn, except that Unionists were good allies for the Conservatives against the Liberals. As ever, it was the politicians who got the Catholics and the Protestants going at each other at the end of the 1800s." So what is often interpreted as religious conflict may be rooted in politics.

It is quite clear that both Catholic and Protestant people in the north consider themselves to be deeply Irish. Rhonda Paisley, daughter of the extreme Loyalist politician and minister, Ian Paisley, explains her own complicated sense of Irish identity: "My culture is Protestant and British, but the most important part is my Irishness. It's more important to me than my Britishness." Grace Doone, a teacher, reflects: "We are a little island, and there is still an awareness of that. There is a concept of Ireland that we all share." Reverend Moore jokingly adds, "I may not be representative, but let's be honest—put me in England and I would be a fish out of water."

Northern Ireland's Antrim Coast

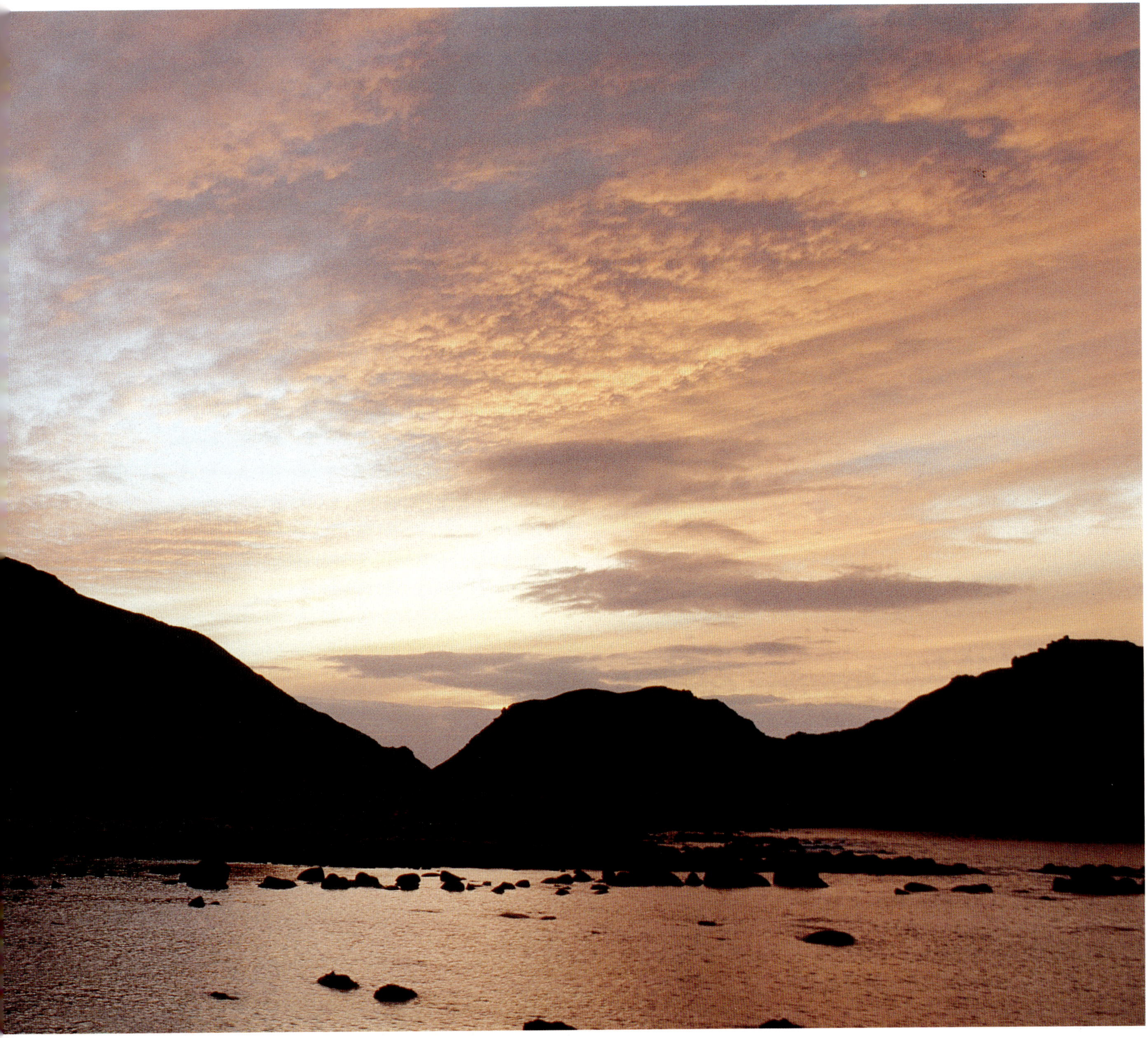

Shipyards

The Harland & Wolff shipyard—featured on the northern Irish five-pound note—is a symbol of Belfast's industrial prosperity at the height of Great Britain's strength as a maritime nation. During the Second World War, the yard's builders worked around the clock to produce battleships for the Royal Navy. It was also in this shipyard that the doomed Titanic and its sister ship were built.

With the decline of shipbuilding in Great Britain and the nationalization of Harland & Wolff, the British government granted to shipyards subsidies amounting to millions of pounds; since the workers were primarily Protestant, many would argue that these funds were to reward Protestants with jobs. Ken Morgan, the British-born manager of Harland & Wolff, adds: "The most important thing to understand about shipbuilding in Belfast is the social implication. If I were an orthodox Christian, I would say that 'the devil finds work for idle hands.' A shipyard in Belfast is unusually important in that it provides a major means of employment. Without employment, social difficulties would be heightened."

The Harland and Wolff Shipyards in East Belfast

Today, the yards are half-empty and the work force depleted, and the British government is no longer willing to bankroll a declining industry. Says Morgan, "We have to consider privatization now because we're interested in survival." Dave Wilson, a welding engineer, acknowledges that it would be a disaster if the shipyard went down. "It's the flagship of this industry," Wilson says. "This shipyard has always been here in East Belfast—125 years in existence. At one time, it employed twenty-four thousand. Now we're down to three thousand!"

TOP: *Rhonda Paisley, Protestant and a Belfast city councilor: "I have a duty to put my education to good use."*

ABOVE: *Reverend Brian Moore of the Shankill Presbyterian Church: "We Protestants are the talk of the world because we are not communicating our faith by the way we live."*

Belfast

As passionate as she is about her "Irishness," Rhonda Paisley is equally committed to her work. A Belfast city councilor, she lives in her parents' home, carefully protected by a full-time security guard. "One of my most important jobs in the Belfast City Council is to oppose the right of Sinn Fein [the political party linked to the IRA] to be with us in the Council. While the British government won't meet with them, they expect us to sit in the same council chamber. We are expected to talk with them while our friends are being murdered. Now that we have direct rule from Westminster, the authority has been taken from us and given to the British Army."

On the subject of integrated schooling—another issue over which there is much controversy—Rhonda is just as serious: "A lot of money is being poured into integrated education, and it affects middle-class families who mix anyway. At the same time, money is being withdrawn in the working-class area, and schools are closing. I don't think you should bus kids from [Catholic] West Belfast. That's disruption. And I feel the Protestant emphasis should be lifted out of state schools."

Having completed an arts course at an American university, Rhonda is also a part-time artist. But it is clear where her priorities lie at the moment: "With a father like mine, how can I sit back and paint? I have a duty to put my education to good use." She adds, "I attend my father's church, the Free Presbyterian Church. What matters most to me is my personal relationship with Christ."

It is slogans such as "Christ for Ulster" in Reverend Paisley's church that perhaps upset traditional Presbyterians such as Reverend Brian Moore, who operates from a church on the Shankill Road bordering the Catholic Falls area. "In Northern Ireland," he remarks, "we suffer from a surfeit of shallow gospelism. Unless our faith is lived out in our lives, it is going to make no impact. We

Protestants are the talk of the world because we are not communicating our faith by the way we live. Take [Reverend Ian] Paisley—he says, 'My way or else. The Church of Rome is the source of all your problems.' The Pope was going to speak at the EEC, and, of course, Paisley voiced his objections. I don't want to talk about his daughter; I would guess she's a chip off the old block, but I don't know.

Reverend Moore has reason to quarrel with Reverend Paisley, who leads the Ulster Unionist Party. Moore devotes much of his time to keeping young Protestant men from joining terrorist paramilitary groups such as the UDR (Ulster Defense Regiment) and the UVF (Ulster Volunteer Force), both of which sympathize with Paisley's party. "A lot of the youngsters take up arms to fight against the IRA," Moore says. "But now disillusionment has set in with some of them; they find it very difficult to break loose because of the pressure placed on them.

"We've actually had to hide some of them in our home for a fortnight and then send them over to England, just to get them out of the clutches of the paramilitaries. One boy was very impressed by the friendship shown him over the years by some of the church leaders. It made him want to change his life. So, of course, they came knocking on his door and wanted him to get involved in some of the jobs that they were doing. We got him off to England where he found a job."

In 1969, British troops were first sent into Belfast after

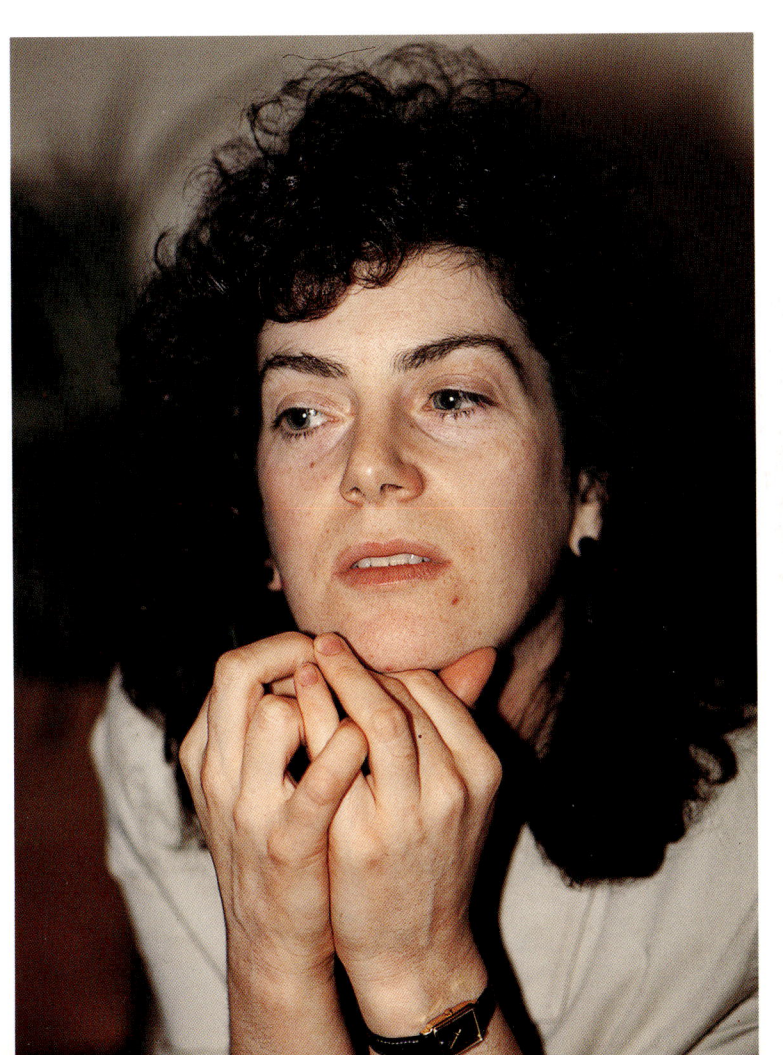

ABOVE: *Father Alec Reid of the Clonard Monastery: "In a situation of conflict, the Church must get into the middle of it and fasten on to what is true. You must feel deeply with both sides."*

LEFT: *Geraldine McAteer, Catholic and mother of two: "Living in Belfast, you're always on edge. If you're stopped late at night, you have your answers ready."*

Loyalists attacked the Catholic minority in West Belfast. Bombay Street was bombed, burned, and rebuilt and is now divided from the Protestant Shankill area by the so-called Peace Line. Around this time, Reverend Moore began a lasting friendship with Father Alec Reid at nearby Clonard Monastery. He recalls: "Alec and I had been drawn together during the 'troubles'—that is, the last twenty years. We used to have meetings twice a month, Protestants and Catholics, to talk over problems. We'd say, 'So-and-so got a brick through his window. Can you do anything about it on your side?' Alec would report what was going on on his side. But we don't have meetings now. Some of us have tried to work together and did what we could, but we got blackballed for it, accused of taking the other side."

Father Alec Reid is understandably reluctant to draw attention to himself: "A priest is a private person, a confidante. The less he appears, the more effective he is. You can undermine your position if you talk to the Press."

On March 6, 1988, Father Reid came to the attention of the world when he was photographed giving last rites to two British soldiers who had been killed while entering a Republican funeral in West Belfast. "I misread the situation," he recalls. "I honestly didn't think that the soldiers would get shot. I thought there would be time to intervene. I genuinely thought they were being taken outside the city for interrogation. I was getting into my car when I heard the shooting. I will always remember a woman crying, 'Oh, Jesus.' There was nobody else there, and one of them was still breathing. The other was dead. My feeling was that I wasn't quick enough. It's easy to be wise after the event.

"It always seems to be women who are around. Two or three women came up behind me, and I turned to them and asked if anyone could do mouth-to-mouth resuscita-

ABOVE AND OPPOSITE RIGHT: *IRA strongholds in Belfast*

tion. They just shook their heads; they were too frightened. So I did it. I kept at it, but the one stopped breathing. I anointed them. Then these two women came up to me. One of them put a coat over his head and said, 'Lord have mercy on him. He was somebody's son.'"

Father Reid has anointed several British soldiers over the years. "I remember," he says, "coming from Dublin one day and seeing a man in a Protestant area who had been killed by a big container lorry. I picked up his Bible and said to myself, 'He must be Protestant.' Then a Protestant man came up with three or four others and insisted that I anoint the dead man. 'How do you know it's his Bible?' he asked. 'You don't know who he is so you better do your duty.' They were going to make sure that I did it, ordering me really, even though I was showing them evidence that he wasn't Catholic."

All of Ireland had been ruled by Britain until 1921 when the southern twenty-six counties became independent, and known as the Irish Free State. The remaining six counties had their own parliament directly under the British Parliament. Northern Ireland is often referred to as Ulster, while the south is now known as the Republic of Ireland.

"In 1916, Republican traditions meant that if you wanted to free Ireland, you had to use force. As the saying went, 'An ounce of dynamite is worth a ton of bladderskite [idle talk].' But the Church must always respond wherever there is injustice. It is not the Christian way for people to settle their differences by war. In a conflict, the Church must get into the middle of it and fasten onto what is true. You must feel deeply with both sides.

"There is a political conflict," comments Father Reid, "between the Nationalists, who want Ireland to be independent, and the Unionists, who want the north to be united with Britain. I don't think that integrated educa-

LEFT AND OPPOSITE RIGHT: *Catholic murals in West Belfast*

tion can really solve it, because it is not a religious conflict.

"For those who believe in the Christian message of justice and love, there can be only one way to peace: the one which recognizes that people are people—God's sons and daughters—before they are Irish, British, Nationalists, Unionists or Republicans."

Geraldine McAteer, mother of two and full-time worker for the Falls Development Committee, is trying to lure outside funds into Catholic West Belfast. With unemployment presently running over 50 percent, she puts the situation into historical perspective: "Initially, Catholics—many of them women and children—found work in the mills. As the city was being built, laboring jobs

OPPOSITE: *Funeral procession in the Fall's Road area of West Belfast*

St. Patrick's Day Mass, Belfast

were available for the Catholic men, whereas the Protestant workers were involved in trades such as shipbuilding, which required skill. Catholic workers did not get in. In 1922, when the new government was set up, even the British Prime Minister said that he would not employ a Catholic because they were not to be trusted. He was running a Protestant party, and he urged other Protestants to employ Protestants. Now, when the owners and those in charge of industry are Protestant, where does a Catholic get a job?"

Geraldine's life has been shaped by this conflict. "When I went to university in Dublin," she explains, "I found it very difficult to mix with people who came from perfectly normal backgrounds. We were normal people living in a very abnormal situation. We've been through a lot of hard years." Unlike many of her educated contemporaries who emigrated to Britain or even America, Geraldine returned to live in Belfast. "I have always felt that anything I learned I should put to use back here. My sister was arrested when she was seventeen, and she was interned [jailed without trial]. There wasn't a damned thing we could do about it. She won't come out until she is forty-one.

"When I was at university, I organized a meeting with

mothers of sons in prison, and they brought tiny letters rolled up in cigarette papers. I got a letter from a former friend in prison, and I read it out loud to an audience of about one hundred people. When I came to the part about prisoners spreading excrement on the walls, I had to stop reading. I was mortified.

"Up until March 31, 1976, people like my sister who were arrested had political status. They were considered political prisoners and could wear their own clothes. But after 1976, political status ended. In the same jail were men with political status and men without it. They wouldn't wear uniforms, only blankets. They weren't allowed books or recreation. They had to run the gauntlet in order to go to the toilet, which meant that excrement collected in their cells. They never washed themselves or brushed their teeth for years on end. One of the prisoners, Bobby Sands, calling for the return of political status, was elected to Parliament while still in prison in a landslide victory. They still let him die on a hunger strike."

Geraldine vividly recalls her only experience in England; it left her shaken and unlikely ever to return: "I had been to college and enjoyed myself. I made a lot of friends, smoked cigarettes, drank, and partied most of the time. Then in 1975, I went off to Amsterdam to work for the summer. We had to take a boat back through England in order to get the train home. An officer said there was a problem with my passport. I had traveled to America when I was a kid, so I knew there was nothing wrong with it. I started to panic. Then they looked through my luggage without my permission and said, 'You know what we're looking for.' The next thing I knew, this policewoman came into the room and said, 'Take your clothes off. You're going to be searched. If you don't cooperate and remove your clothes, there's a man outside who will do it for you.' I was held for five days. It was because my sister was interned and I was Irish. It was hell. I never felt more alone."

181

Brendan Lister, 35, with his son on the porch of their house. In the background, the wire mesh of the "Peace Line" is visible. The mesh is to protect their home and others on Bombay Street from firebombs.

Outside the Clonard Monastery, Lorraine Lister, thirty-three and mother of four, pointed to a nondescript terraced house where, only a week before, a Loyalist knocked down the back door and shot a man while neighbors stood by helplessly. "We can't defend ourselves. If a Loyalist gets caught with a gun, he gets a six-month sentence. A Catholic gets twenty years!"

On the night of July 13th, the tiny street on which the Lister family lives exploded in Loyalist wrath. "Sure as Almighty God," recalls Lorraine, "about two in the morning we got the first burst of heavy fire. It went on until about five, and then the peelers [police] started searching houses. The police shot at the firemen on our street instead of at the Prods [Protestants] who were petrol-bombing and shooting. They raided this side of the Peace Line, saying that the Prods had complained of stones. Why didn't they stop them throwing bombs?

"We always get trouble in the Marching Season—June, July, and August. They commemorate William of Orange's defeat of King James, who was Catholic. July 12th is always the big demo. They light the bonfires as near to us as possible. In August 1969, the Loyalists burned parts of Belfast. The RUC [Royal Ulster Constabulary] led them in and stood by while it all burnt down. Money was collected from all over the world and a lot of people moved back in. Even with 'the troubles,' we feel safer here in our own wee enclaves. The Catholic people of the Ardoyne would give their eyeteeth to move here."

Most people would find it hard to believe that anyone would want to change places with the Lister family. Lorraine's husband Brendan and his brother Ray have both been unemployed for over ten years. "I went to work when I was sixteen," recalls Ray, "down in the Falls [a Catholic area] where there were lots of linen mills. The Loyalists got the mills burned down, and a thousand jobs went up in smoke. After that, I could only get laboring or building jobs."

With no earned income, the family depends on the dwindling British welfare state. Each of the six family members gets about £9.10, or $13.94, per week. This is supposed to cover all the necessities, including electricity, coal, food, clothes, and transport. Rent amounts to $14.40 per week for their government-owned house. Because of the children, Lorraine gets another $48.80 in family allowance. "You always owe money before you get a check," remarks Lorraine. "Brendan and I have been married for thirteen years, and we've had one holiday."

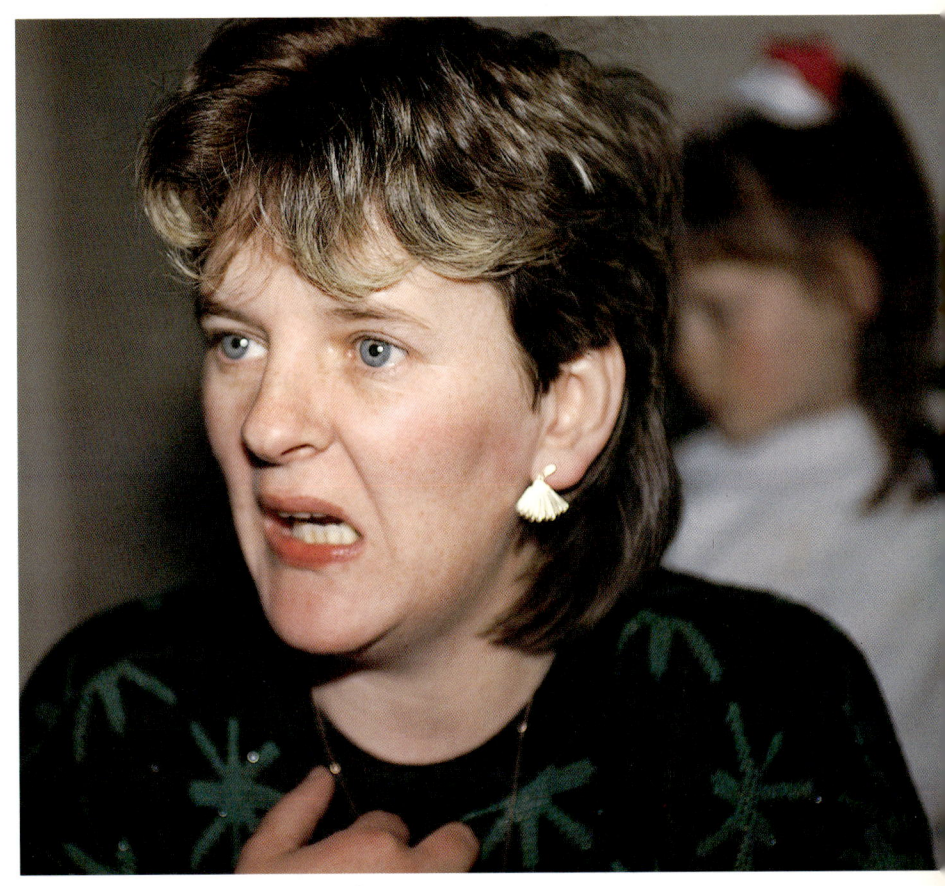

Lorraine Lister, 33. "You don't know what it's like to live here on the edge, in fear all the time. You get used to it."

LEFT: *Brendan Lister. "I went to the shipyard, and they asked me what school I went to. I said, 'St. Peter's,' which is Catholic. They said, 'Sorry, no job. It's been filled.'"*

Paul Caulfield, now eighteen, is a graduate of every juvenile penal institution in Belfast. "My parents," he explains, "separated when I was six. When I was thirteen, I left my Mum to live with my Dad. With three sisters, I felt I was the only man in the house and that they were all against me. My stepmother, Margaret, was a Protestant but was always very kind to me. When I was fifteen, some men came into the house through the back window. I heard shots in the room next door. Margaret was killed—I guess because she was living with a Catholic. My father was also shot but not dead. I was angry and scared. We had no phone, so I went to the neighbors. Afterwards, my mother came and got me. She and Margaret were friends. That was three years ago and I never got over it."

Paul went to a Catholic primary school, where, he says, "I came to realize that there were two sides. I grew up thinking I was better than them. When I was about eleven, I broke into a house three times. The police called up, and I admitted that I'd done it and that I didn't know any better. That was the first time I was in a police station. I was put on probation.

"Later on, I got caught breaking all the windows in a Protestant church around midnight. I was put in St. Patrick's Training School. At thirteen, I was thrown out of high school because they said I had a knife down someone's back. Then I got put into a secure unit for breaking into cars. We started a riot there."

Paul Caulfield, age 18, Catholic resident of Belfast. Paul points to the place where his Protestant stepmother was shot. She was killed for living with a Catholic.

According to one social worker, even being a child in Belfast is risky: "In a one-day census, 18 percent of the children in detention had never committed an offense. They could go in for not attending school. With a Training School Order, young people can be taken away from their homes as young as ten. These training schools are locked units that operate an informal justice system. They are dead strict. Paul spent three days 'on the board'—locked in his cell twenty-three hours a day. The children have to scrub floors, and they can't step on the white tiles. Paul was punched in the face for not calling a guard 'Sir.'"

With some of his troubles behind him, Paul is now on a full-time Youth Training Scheme (YTS) doing metal work. For this, the government pays him $56, of which Paul gives $24 to his grandmother for housekeeping.

Mill Strand Primary School

"I have always been very proud to say that I am Irish," says Hylda Armstrong. "I feel Irish. I just happen to live in one of the six counties that are in the north of Ireland."

Ironically, if anyone deserves to harbor resentment toward others, it is Hylda. "Both my grandparents were southern Irish and had to leave because they were Protestants living in a predominantly Roman Catholic area." Yet, because her parents were "very tolerant people," Hylda has devoted much of her life to bringing Protestants and Catholics together. Widowed very young, Hylda suffered a second tragedy when her son Sean was killed for his efforts to set up integrated holiday camps for Belfast children.

"Sean spent six years working his way around the world. He came back because Ireland was in trouble. As the first field officer for the International Voluntary Service for Northern Ireland, he used his own home in Belfast as a place for children to meet—Roman Catholic and Protestant together. My son had just married a lovely little American girl. They went off to Scotland for their honeymoon and came back on a Friday evening. He had three hundred children leaving the next morning. A young man came to the door and asked, 'Are you Robert Sean Armstrong?' And Sean, thinking that the man was a parent, said, 'Yes.' But he wasn't a parent. He pulled a gun and shot Sean.

"We don't even belong to a political party. Sean's life was taken by someone with a sick, twisted mind. He

Hylda Armstrong, whose son was killed for his efforts to bring Protestant and Catholic children together

only knew that Sean stood for togetherness."

In memory of her slain son, Hylda has worked over the years to establish Glebe House, a holiday camp for both Protestant and Catholic children. She is also credited with the establishment of the integrated Mill Strand Primary School in Portrush on the northern coast. Hylda is modest about her role: "It was at the request of parents in this area. The balance of Protestant and Catholic is fifty-fifty—some with no religion at all. Very often, Protestant schools taught British history with a little bit of Irish, and Roman Catholic schools taught Irish history with a little bit of British. Communication has to come at an early age, because children are the future of this country and the world. The children should learn, at least, to listen to one another's thinking. Then they can say, 'Yes, that might be all right, but I will still retain what I believe.' Unfortunately, some of these children come from households with very strong ways of thinking, and some will say exactly what their parents say. For instance, one little boy told me, 'Get the Brits out.' Then he looked at me and said, 'But I don't mean the Irish Brits.' I'm very confident about the future of integrated education, but it's going to be a long, hard struggle, because our schools are not funded. Money does not come easily.

"This latest upheaval has lasted over twenty years, and did not even start as a religious division. It was really political and economic. But I think it is wrong if we allow ourselves to become immune to suffering. We must still feel for other people. I still listen to the midnight news and hope, 'Please God, don't let anyone have suffered.'"

Desmond Irwin, Principal of the Mill Strand School

LEFT AND PAGES 188-190: *Children at the Mill Strand Primary School in Portrush, Northern Ireland*

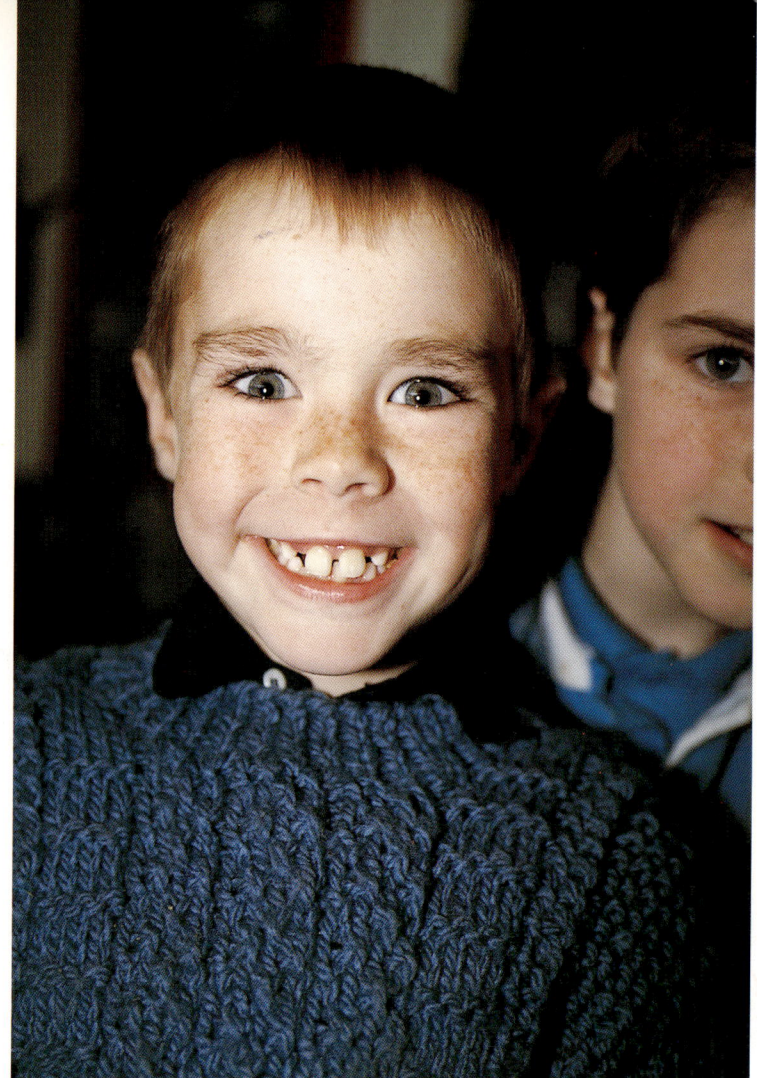

"I think there's more pressure on Catholic parents because of the Church. I went and talked to my local priest about what provisions there would be for my son, who was going to Mill Strand. He said that as a Catholic I was obliged to send my child to a Catholic school and that Peter couldn't receive the sacraments of Holy Communion and Confirmation in this church. As it was explained to me, one of the reasons that the Church keeps the Catholic schools is because they really feel that the Irish identity in the north is under threat."

—BERNICE MARTINS, *Catholic parent*

"Irish was long recognized by the British Department of Education as a modern language. Now they have removed its status and demoted it to cultural studies. I'm not opposed to integrated education, but I'm not happy about it either. It's as though some stood and fought while others went off to the Welsh hills to form communes—they don't challenge the system; it's only an alternative for a small group."

—BERNADETTE (DEVLIN) MCALISKEY,
former Member of Parliament and mother of three

"We start very small in my classroom every morning. We get the children in the room thinking, 'I feel sorry that I hurt someone else, and I have forgiven someone who hurt me.' That is very important. Each person has to begin with the heart and spread it out—like the trunk and branches of a tree."

—Grace Doone, *Mill Strand teacher*

Acknowledgments

Portrait of Great Britain and Northern Ireland was inspired by the four-part television series, *Portrait of Great Britain*, produced by Turner Broadcasting System, Inc. and aired on TBS in 1990.

There are several people at TBS who made this book possible. I would like to thank personally Ted Turner, Ira Miskin, John Savage and Merle Worth, who produced and developed the series. Also, Liza Levine, Tracy A. Mitchell, Nonny Majchrzyk, Miles Ross, and Jude Allen were extremely helpful.

While this book is organized geographically, the television series was divided into the following categories: *This Sceptered Isle, Empire, Society,* and *True Brit*. Each program was produced by a different group of people, and I would like to credit those not already mentioned.

On *This Sceptered Isle:* Judy Towers Reemstma, Gary M. Steele, Terry Hopkins, and David Wateilston.

On *Empire:* David Gerrard, Wally Plummer, and Russ T. Fisher.

On *Society:* Helen Whitney, Leslie Karsten, and Doug Dunderdale.

On *True Brit:* Witold Starecki and Ted Winterburn.

A word of thanks to Monica Griswold, Lisa Saylan, Cecilia Harrington, Lisa Oliver, Becky Butler, Jason Williams, and Jane Quigley.

Most importantly, I would like to thank Bridget Ann Bennett for her research, guidance and support, especially in Northern Ireland. Without her help, I would not have been able to take the photographs in this book.

—MICHAEL REAGAN, *January 3, 1990*

N

| 0 | 50 | 100 | 150 | Km. |
| 0 | 50 | | 100 | Mi. |